BEYOND VANILLA

ART OF BUILDING UNIQUE AND EXCEPTIONAL BRANDS

SHAGUN JAIN

Made with ♥ on the Notion Press Platform
www.notionpress.com

Contents

About The Author *v*

Acknowledgements *vii*

Preface *ix*

The Foundations Of Exceptional Branding

1. Introduction: Beyond Vanilla Thinking 3
2. The Vanilla Trap 9
3. What Makes A Brand Exceptional? 19

The Core Elements Of Differentiation

4. Discovering Your Brand's Core Identity 33
5. Differentiation Strategies 41
6. The Visual And Verbal Identity 51

Designing Exceptional Brand Experiences

7. From Product To Experience 59
8. The Role Of Emotional Branding 64
9. Personalization At Scale 70

Mastering The Art Of Disruption

10. Challenging Industry Norms 85
11. Leveraging Innovation For Uniqueness 93
12. Sustainability And Social Impact 99

Growth Strategies For Long-Term Success

13. Consistency Vs. Evolution 109
14. The Role Of Customer Engagement 116
15. Marketing Beyond The Noise 122

The Psychology And Science Of Branding

16. The Neuroscience Of Branding 131
17. The Power Of Emotional Triggers 136

Contents

18. Cultural And Behavioral Insights 142

Building A Legacy Of Distinction

19. The Beyond Vanilla Manifesto 147

20. Future-Proofing Your Brand 150

21. Crafting Your Brand's Legacy 154

Brand Story: MyFroyoland

Worksheets and Exercises for Immediate Action 165

Other Books by the Author 169

About The Author

Shagun Jain is a dynamic professional with a passion for storytelling, branding, and business. An MBA graduate with a specialization in Marketing from Flame University, Pune, Shagun has honed expertise in brand management, luxury branding, and the art of creating unique, memorable brand identities.

Beyond the classroom, Shagun brings a rich legacy of entrepreneurship to the table, rooted in a family jewellery business. This background instilled a deep appreciation for tradition, craftsmanship, and the importance of building lasting connections with customers. Today, Shagun seamlessly blends this heritage with modern marketing insights, offering a rare perspective that bridges the old and the new.

In addition to being a jeweller and marketer, Shagun is also a writer. As the author of *Gold vs The Indian Stock Market: History and the Way Forward*, Shagun has delved into the fascinating intersection of precious metals and financial markets, exploring their historical significance and future potential.

This book, *Beyond Vanilla: Art of Building Unique and Exceptional Brands*, reflects Shagun's deep understanding of what it takes to stand out in a crowded marketplace. With a flair for creativity and a keen eye for detail, Shagun inspires readers to embrace bold ideas, push boundaries, and leave a lasting impression in the ever-evolving world of branding.

When not immersed in brand strategies or penning thought-provoking books, Shagun enjoys exploring the nuances of luxury craftsmanship, connecting with creative minds, and finding inspiration in the stories of people and businesses daring to be different.

Acknowledgements

Writing this book has been an extraordinary journey, and I owe its existence to the support, encouragement, and inspiration of many incredible people who have stood by me along the way.

First and foremost, my heartfelt gratitude goes to my family. Your unwavering belief in me, even when I was knee-deep in drafts and consumed by ideas, gave me the strength to keep going.

To my professors and mentors, thank you for being a guiding light throughout my journey. Your wisdom, insights, and encouragement have been instrumental in shaping my perspective on branding and creativity. The lessons you've imparted continue to resonate in my work, and this book reflects the foundation you helped me build.

To my friends and colleagues—thank you for being my sounding boards, my cheerleaders, and my critics. Your insights, feedback, and enthusiasm pushed me to dig deeper and aim higher.

I am deeply thankful to the creative professionals, entrepreneurs, and dreamers who inspired this book. Your stories of daring to be different, of pushing boundaries and challenging norms, have been the heartbeat of these pages.

Finally, to the readers—you are the reason this book exists. Whether you're building a brand, refining an idea, or simply seeking inspiration, you are the ones who dare to go beyond vanilla. Thank you for choosing to join me on this journey. Your trust and curiosity fuel my passion for storytelling and creativity.

To all of you—thank you. This book is as much yours as it is mine. Let's make the world a little more remarkable, one bold idea at a time.

With gratitude,

Shagun Jain

Preface

In a world bursting with ideas, brands, and noise, standing out feels harder than ever. The landscape is crowded, the competition is fierce, and the pressure to be different is overwhelming. But here's the truth: building an extraordinary brand isn't about shouting louder or following trends. It's about going *beyond vanilla*—moving past the ordinary and daring to be exceptional in a world that's quick to settle for average.

This book is your guide to doing just that. It's not a step-by-step manual; it's a rallying cry, a toolbox, and a source of inspiration for brands that want to leave their mark. Whether you're building a brand from scratch or looking to breathe new life into an established one, this book will help you uncover what makes you truly unique and show you how to use that uniqueness as your superpower.

We'll explore everything from the neuroscience of branding to the power of emotional triggers, dive into cultural insights that align your brand with the times, and even uncover how to craft a legacy that will endure for generations. Along the way, you'll find practical tools, thought-provoking exercises, and real-world examples that will challenge you to think differently and push boundaries.

But let's be clear: this isn't about chasing perfection or ticking boxes. This is about embracing your brand's quirks, amplifying your strengths, and creating something so memorable that it's impossible to ignore. It's about crafting a brand that doesn't just sell but connects—on an emotional, cultural, and human level.

As you turn these pages, get ready to challenge norms, take bold risks, and fall in love with the process of building something extraordinary. Because the world doesn't need another cookie-cutter brand. It needs your brand—raw, real, and remarkable.

Welcome to the journey of going *beyond vanilla*. It's time to be unforgettable.

Let's get started.

The Foundations of Exceptional Branding

CHAPTER ONE

Introduction: Beyond Vanilla Thinking

Let's face it—vanilla is... fine. It's safe, it's predictable, it's that flavor you pick when you're not feeling adventurous. But does anyone ever rave about vanilla? "Oh my gosh, you HAVE to try this vanilla!" Yeah, didn't think so. Vanilla is the comfort zone of branding—a place where too many businesses hang out, hoping to please everyone and not ruffle any feathers. The problem? Playing it safe might keep you in the game, but it won't make you a star.

Why Brands Need to Break Free from the Ordinary?

Safe is Boring

Sure, staying in the safe zone feels cozy. But in a world where consumers are bombarded with thousands of brands, safe also means forgettable. Do you want people to look at your brand and think, "Oh, yeah, that's nice, I guess"? Or do you want them to think, "Wow, this is incredible—I need to tell everyone about it!" Spoiler: It's the second one.

People Want More Than Just Products

Look, people aren't just buying stuff anymore—they're buying feelings, stories, and a little slice of something special. They want brands that get them, brands that feel like an extension of their personality. If your brand screams "meh," why should they care? Breaking free from the ordinary means adding that spark that makes people stop, notice, and feel connected.

Standing Out Isn't Optional Anymore

Picture this: You're at a party, and everyone's wearing the same plain white t-shirt. Then someone walks in wearing a bold, colorful outfit, owning the room. That's the power of standing out! In a crowded market, being different isn't just nice—it's essential. If you don't want to fade into the background, you've got to bring something unique to the table.

Taking Risks Pays Off (Eventually)

Okay, sure, stepping out of your comfort zone can feel like jumping off a cliff. But here's the thing—brands like Apple, Tesla, and Nike didn't become legends by playing it safe. They took bold risks, made some people uncomfortable, and built empires because they dared to do what others wouldn't. Playing it safe might keep you afloat, but being bold is what makes waves.

Ordinary is the Fast Lane to Obscurity

Let's not sugarcoat it: If your brand doesn't stand out, it's not going to survive. The world moves fast, trends change faster, and customers have zero patience for bland. If you're not evolving, you're becoming irrelevant—and nobody wants that.

What Does It Mean to Go Beyond Vanilla?

This book isn't about adding a sprinkle of cinnamon to your plain old vanilla brand. It's about ditching the safe flavor entirely and creating something so exciting, so magnetic, that people can't stop talking about it. Going beyond vanilla means thinking differently, taking risks, and embracing what makes your brand uniquely you.

The good news? You don't have to figure this out alone. This book is your guide to turning your brand into something extraordinary. Whether you're just starting out or ready to shake things up, we're going to dive into the strategies, stories, and ideas that will take your brand from ordinary to unforgettable.

So, let's leave vanilla behind, shall we? The world's ready for something bold, and so are you. Let's get to it!

The Promise of Uniqueness in a Crowded Market

Imagine walking into a packed room where everyone's talking at once. Some voices are loud, others are soft, but after a while, it all blends into a single, indistinguishable hum. Then, out of nowhere, someone starts singing your favorite song, and suddenly, they have your full attention. That's the magic of uniqueness in a crowded market—it's the one voice that rises above the noise, making people stop, listen, and care.

In today's world, standing out isn't just a nice-to-have; it's a survival skill. Here's why embracing your brand's uniqueness is like unlocking a superpower:

Why Uniqueness Matters More Than Ever?

Standing Out in a Saturated Market

The Indian market is competitive. From tier-1 cities to rural areas, brands are fighting for consumer mindshare. In this battle, blending in is the fastest way to be ignored. Uniqueness ensures you're not just another option but the option.

Example: Paper Boat

Paper Boat transformed the beverage market by focusing on nostalgia. Instead of competing with carbonated drinks, they reintroduced traditional Indian drinks like aam panna and jaljeera, paired with minimalist packaging and emotional storytelling. Their uniqueness wasn't just in the product but in the experience of reliving childhood memories.

Building Emotional Loyalty

Indian consumers are deeply emotional when it comes to brands. They're drawn to stories, values, and products that resonate with their culture and aspirations. When a brand taps into this emotional connection, it creates loyalty that goes beyond transactions.

Example: Amul

Amul didn't just market dairy products—it became the "Taste of India." Their long-standing cartoon advertisements, filled with wit and commentary on current events, struck a chord with millions, making Amul a household name for generations.

Competing Beyond Price

The Indian market is price-sensitive, but uniqueness allows brands to move beyond price wars. A distinct product or experience gives consumers a reason to pay a premium.

Example: Tata Tea (Jaago Re Campaign)

Tata Tea didn't just sell tea; they sold a message of social awakening with their "Jaago Re" campaign. By connecting their product to social responsibility, they elevated their brand and commanded a loyal, conscious consumer base.

Indian Brands That Prove Uniqueness Wins

- ***Fabindia***

Fabindia turned Indian handwoven textiles into a lifestyle brand. By blending traditional craftsmanship with modern designs, they appealed to urban consumers seeking authenticity. Their stores offer not just clothes but an experience of India's heritage, making them a go-to brand for ethical and stylish fashion.

- *Royal Enfield*

In a market dominated by commuter bikes, Royal Enfield positioned itself as a symbol of rugged individuality. Their vintage-inspired motorcycles, coupled with a strong community-driven brand ethos, turned their bikes into aspirational products for adventure enthusiasts.

- *Zomato*

Zomato didn't just deliver food—it built a personality. With quirky, relatable social media posts and a focus on hyper-localized experiences, they became more than just a service provider; they became a brand people loved engaging with.

- *Nykaa*

Nykaa revolutionized the beauty and personal care segment in India by combining e-commerce with personalized beauty solutions. By curating a wide range of products and focusing on empowering women, they created a brand that felt relatable and aspirational.

- *Chumbak*

Chumbak carved its niche in the lifestyle space with quirky, colorful designs inspired by Indian motifs. By creating products that were both functional and playful, they appealed to young, urban consumers looking for something fresh and fun.

How Uniqueness Creates Opportunity

When a brand embraces what makes it different, it shifts the conversation. Uniqueness allows you to:

- **Command attention in a crowded space.**
- **Build emotional connections with your audience.**
- **Create a sense of exclusivity and aspirational value.**
- **Turn customers into advocates who champion your brand.**

The Bigger Promise of Uniqueness

In India's vibrant, ever-changing market, the promise of uniqueness is not just about survival—it's about thriving. It's about daring to stand apart, crafting a story that resonates, and offering something that feels irreplaceable.

Uniqueness isn't just a strategy; it's a commitment. It's a promise to your audience that you're not here to blend in but to create something they can truly connect with. And as the examples above show, when you deliver on that promise, the rewards are extraordinary.

So, here's the real question: Are you ready to go beyond vanilla and embrace what makes your brand remarkable?

CHAPTER TWO

THE VANILLA TRAP

The Dangers of Playing It Safe

Playing it safe might feel like the responsible thing to do. After all, vanilla has its charm—it's familiar, dependable, and appeals to almost everyone. But here's the catch: in today's fast-paced, ultra-competitive market, "safe" often translates to "forgettable." **The Vanilla Trap** is the pitfall brands fall into when they try to please everyone, blend in, and avoid risks. It might keep you afloat for a while, but it won't help you thrive.

Let's dig into why playing it safe can be more dangerous than you think.

Vanilla Blends In (and That's Not a Good Thing) -- The biggest issue with being "vanilla" is that you disappear into the crowd. When your brand is just like everyone else's—same messaging, same visuals, same promises—it's nearly impossible to stand out. People don't remember brands that feel generic; they remember the ones that dared to be different.

- Think about the sea of budget smartphones in the Indian market. Brands that rely solely on features like "affordable price" or "great battery life" without unique branding or an emotional connection often struggle to gain traction against standouts like **Xiaomi** or **OnePlus**, which pair functionality with a distinct identity.

Playing It Safe Kills Innovation -- When you stick to what's been done before, you're not innovating—you're imitating. The problem? Consumers are always looking for something fresh, exciting, and different. Playing it safe keeps your brand stuck in the past, while bolder competitors are already defining the future.

- Take the airline industry in India. For years, most airlines operated with standard, no-frills services. Then came **IndiGo**, which revolutionized the experience by focusing on simplicity, punctuality, and efficient service delivery. Their bold blue branding and clear messaging set them apart from the rest.

Safe Brands Struggle to Build Loyalty -- Playing it safe often means trying to appeal to everyone. But when you dilute your brand to the point where it's all things to all people, it loses its identity. Brands that don't stand for something specific fail to create an emotional connection, and without that, loyalty is hard to come by.

- Compare **Tata Tea's "Jaago Re"** campaign, which resonated deeply with socially conscious consumers, to generic tea brands that simply tout "great taste." One inspires loyalty; the other is easily replaceable.

Price Becomes the Only Differentiator -- When your brand doesn't stand out for its personality, innovation, or story, you're left competing on price. This race to the bottom is not sustainable, especially in markets like India, where margins are already thin.

- The flood of cookie-cutter clothing brands on e-commerce platforms often rely on heavy discounts to attract buyers. In contrast, a brand like **Fabindia**, with its emphasis on heritage and craftsmanship, can charge a premium because of its distinct identity.

You Risk Losing Relevance -- The market evolves quickly, and consumer expectations are always shifting. Brands that stick to a "safe" formula often fail to adapt, making them irrelevant over time. Staying vanilla might keep you comfortable in the short term, but in the long run, it's a surefire way to fade into obscurity.

- Look at how **Havells** transformed from a typical electrical goods company to a household name with innovative ads like "Wires that don't catch fire." They left the vanilla messaging behind and stayed relevant by focusing on emotional safety and trust.

> "***The Trap is Comfortable—But It's Also a Dead End***
> *It's tempting to stick with what's been done before. Safe feels predictable, and predictable feels manageable. But while you're busy avoiding risks, you're also avoiding opportunities. The Vanilla Trap keeps you in a cycle of mediocrity, where your brand is good but never great.*"

How to Escape the Vanilla Trap?

Embrace Boldness

Take risks with your messaging, design, or product offerings. Bold brands get noticed.

Example: Zomato's quirky social media campaigns have become a case study in how bold, relatable content wins over audiences.

Focus on Your Niche

Don't try to be everything for everyone. Pick a niche, own it, and speak directly to that audience.

Example: Mamaearth carved out a niche in toxin-free, eco-friendly skincare, appealing to conscious consumers.

Tell a Story

Build a narrative that connects with your audience on a deeper level. People love stories—they're far more compelling than generic marketing slogans.

Example: Paper Boat's storytelling taps into nostalgia, making their brand feel personal and unique.

Innovate Continuously

Keep pushing the boundaries of what your brand can do. Innovation isn't just about products; it's about how you deliver value.

Example: Swiggy moved beyond food delivery to groceries and convenience services, keeping their brand fresh and relevant.

The Vanilla Trap may seem like a safe bet, but in reality, it's a recipe for getting lost in the crowd. Today's consumers don't just want good—they want extraordinary. They crave brands that stand for something, take risks, and offer something no one else can.

So, if your brand is stuck in the vanilla zone, it's time to shake things up. Add some spice, sprinkle some creativity, and dare to be bold. Because in this competitive world, only those who break free from the ordinary truly thrive.

How Generic Branding Stifles Growth

In today's hyper-competitive marketplace, generic branding is one of the quickest ways to stifle growth. When your brand looks, feels, or sounds like everyone else's, it loses the ability to stand out. Imagine walking down a supermarket aisle filled with products that all promise the same thing—"best quality," "lowest price," or "trusted by millions." Nothing grabs your attention because everything blends into a sea of sameness. This is the fundamental problem with generic branding: it lacks distinction, making it nearly impossible for customers to notice, remember, or care about your brand. Without that recognition, growth becomes an uphill battle.

One of the biggest pitfalls of generic branding is that it forces you to compete solely on price. When your brand doesn't offer anything unique, customers default to the cheapest option, setting off a race to the bottom. This not only hurts profitability but also leaves little room for reinvestment in innovation or marketing. On the other hand, distinct brands can command a premium by offering something more than just a product—an experience, a story, or a sense of identity. For instance, **Tata Salt** distinguished itself in the otherwise generic salt market by positioning itself as **"Desh ka Namak" (The Nation's Salt)**, emphasizing trust and purity. This strong emotional connection allowed them to charge a premium and dominate the category.

Generic branding also prevents the formation of emotional bonds with customers, which are crucial for building loyalty. People are naturally drawn to brands with personality, authenticity, and a compelling story. Without these elements, your brand becomes just another option, easily replaced by the next competitor. Take **Amul**, for example. Instead of simply marketing dairy products, Amul created a lovable brand personality with its witty advertisements and strong association with India's cultural identity. This emotional resonance has made Amul a household name for decades. In contrast, countless other dairy brands that focus solely on functional benefits like "pure milk" struggle to stand out or build loyalty.

Even innovation can fall flat without effective branding. A groundbreaking product might go unnoticed if it's wrapped in a generic identity that fails to communicate its value. For example, **BoAt** emerged as a leader in India's consumer electronics market by combining innovative, stylish headphones with bold, youthful branding. Their distinct identity amplified the impact of their innovation, helping them grow rapidly. In contrast, many similar products from generic brands fade into obscurity, even if they offer comparable features.

Perhaps the most significant danger of generic branding is the long-term loss of relevance. The market evolves rapidly, and consumer expectations shift constantly. Brands that stick to a safe, generic formula risk becoming outdated as bold competitors redefine the industry. Think of **Royal Enfield**, which was once considered a niche brand. Instead of marketing their motorcycles purely as vehicles, they redefined their identity by associating the brand with adventure, freedom, and a rugged lifestyle. This transformation not only attracted a new audience but also created a loyal community of enthusiasts, ensuring their relevance in a competitive market.

Ultimately, generic branding is a growth killer because it fails to inspire, connect, or differentiate. It keeps your brand trapped in mediocrity, fighting for scraps in a crowded market. Breaking free from this trap requires boldness—defining your unique identity, telling a compelling story, and creating a brand that people can relate to and remember. In a world filled with sameness, it's the brands that dare to be different that capture attention, foster loyalty, and achieve sustainable growth. If your brand is stuck in the generic zone, it's time to rethink your strategy and start standing out. That's where true growth begins.

Recognizing When Your Brand Blends In

Imagine walking into a bookshop where every cover looks exactly the same—plain, beige, and uninspired. You glance around, but nothing catches your eye. Eventually, you leave without picking anything up because, well, nothing stood out. That's exactly what happens when a brand blends in: it doesn't excite, it doesn't inspire, and it certainly doesn't stick in anyone's memory. In today's saturated market, blending in is the silent killer for any brand. The good news? Recognizing when your brand is stuck in the sea of sameness is the first step to breaking out and becoming the one that turns heads, sparks curiosity, and earns loyalty. Let's explore the signs and how to infuse your brand with the uniqueness it deserves.

1. Your Messaging is as Generic as Instant Coffee

Let's be honest: if your brand is claiming to have "the best quality" or "trusted by millions," you might as well be whispering in a crowded stadium. These phrases are so overused that they've lost all meaning. Consumers have heard it all before, and generic messaging like this doesn't give them any reason to choose you over your competitors.

Imagine two shops selling mango juice. One says, "Fresh mango juice." The other says, "Relive summer memories with every sip of our Alphonso mango blend." Which one would you pick? Exactly.

What to do: Find your unique voice. Think about what truly sets your brand apart and shout it from the rooftops.

2. Your Visual Identity Screams "Copy-Paste"

Your logo, **colors**, and **design** are the first things people notice about your brand—or don't. If your branding looks like it came from a "Top 10 Free Logos" website, it's probably blending in. Bland visuals make it hard for customers to differentiate you from competitors. Think about how many brands in the FMCG sector use blue and white packaging to scream "clean and trustworthy."

Now, imagine walking into that same aisle and spotting a bright, quirky package with a funky font. That's what BoAt did in the electronics space. Instead of sticking to the dull greys and blacks common in the industry, they embraced bold designs and youthful colors, instantly making their brand memorable.

What to do: Audit your visual identity. Does your logo spark curiosity? Are your colors bold and distinctive? If not, it's time for a makeover.

3. You're Stuck in the Price War

If the only reason customers choose you is because you're the cheapest option, your brand has a serious problem. Competing on price is like running on a treadmill—you're moving, but you're not going anywhere. Sure, you might win some sales in the short term, but you'll lose out in the long run when a competitor undercuts you.

Take a cue from Royal Enfield, which refused to compete with budget motorcycle brands. Instead, they positioned themselves as a premium lifestyle brand for adventurers. By focusing on the experience of freedom and rugged individuality, they created a loyal fan base that's willing to pay a premium.

What to do: Shift the conversation from price to value. Highlight what makes your product or service worth every penny.

4. Your Customers Can't Describe You

Here's a fun challenge: ask five of your customers to describe your brand in one sentence. If their answers are vague, generic, or wildly inconsistent, it's a sign you're blending in. Strong brands leave an impression. If people struggle to articulate what makes your brand special, they probably won't recommend it to others—or remember it themselves.

What to do: Refine your brand story. Give your audience a clear narrative that's easy to remember and share.

5. Your Competitors Look Just Like You

Here's a quick test: swap your logo with a competitor's on your website or marketing materials. If the message still works, you've got a problem. This happens when brands rely too heavily on industry trends instead of carving out their own identity.

For example, think about how Nykaa stood out in the crowded beauty market. While competitors were busy using clichéd imagery of flawless models, Nykaa celebrated diversity and individuality. Their campaigns showcased real people, creating an emotional connection with their audience.

What to do: Study your competitors not to copy them, but to find gaps you can fill. Be the brand that does something no one else is doing.

6. No One Feels Anything When They Interact with Your Brand

If your brand doesn't evoke any emotion—whether it's excitement, trust, or nostalgia—it's not making an impact. Emotions drive decisions, and brands that connect on an emotional level build stronger relationships with their audience.

What to do: Build emotional connections by aligning your brand with values, causes, or stories that resonate with your audience.

7. Your Growth Has Plateaued

If your sales have flatlined despite your marketing efforts, it's likely because your brand isn't standing out. A lack of differentiation makes it difficult to attract new customers or retain existing ones, especially in a competitive market where every business is fighting for attention.

What to do: Revisit your strategy and find ways to reinvigorate your brand. Look at Chumbak, a lifestyle brand that started with quirky souvenirs. By expanding into fashion and home decor while maintaining their playful identity, they managed to stay relevant and grow.

> "***The Danger of Ignoring the Problem***
>
> *The scariest part about blending in is that it often goes unnoticed—until it's too late. It's easy to think, "Our product is great, so people will eventually notice." Spoiler alert: they won't. In today's noisy marketplace, good isn't enough. You have to be remarkable.*
>
> *Ignoring the signs of generic branding can lead to stagnation, declining sales, and eventual irrelevance. The market is filled with stories of brands that failed to evolve and were replaced by bold competitors who weren't afraid to stand out.*"

Breaking Free and Standing Out

If you've realized your brand is blending in, congratulations—you're ahead of the curve. Many businesses stay in denial, convincing themselves that mediocrity is enough. Recognizing the problem is the first step toward solving it.

Here's how to start:

Define Your Unique Value Proposition: Identify what makes your brand truly special and make it the foundation of your messaging.

Embrace Bold Design: Don't be afraid to experiment with colors, fonts, and visuals that make your brand pop.

Tell Your Story: People connect with stories, not products. Share your journey, values, and vision.

Innovate Continuously: Keep finding new ways to add value for your customers.

Build Emotional Connections: Align your brand with causes, emotions, or values that resonate with your audience.

Recognizing when your brand blends in isn't about admitting failure—it's about unlocking potential. Blending in might feel safe, but it's the riskiest thing you can do in a world that rewards the bold and the brave. By acknowledging the signs and taking deliberate steps to stand out, you can transform your brand into something that captures attention, earns loyalty, and drives growth.

So, are you ready to step out of the shadows and make your mark? The world is waiting for your unique story—tell it loud and tell it proud. After all, life's too short to be vanilla.

CHAPTER THREE

WHAT MAKES A BRAND EXCEPTIONAL?

The Pillars of Uniqueness

Think of an exceptional brand as the life of the party. It's the one that walks in, and everyone stops to take notice. It's not just about being loud or flashy; it's about having that certain something—a mix of confidence, personality, and charm that leaves a lasting impression. Exceptional brands don't just sell products or services; they create experiences, inspire loyalty, and carve out their own little corner of people's hearts. But what exactly makes a brand exceptional? At its core, it's all about embracing uniqueness, and that uniqueness stands tall on a few key pillars.

A Clear Purpose: Your Brand's North Star

Every exceptional brand starts with a purpose. It's the "why" behind what you do—the reason your brand exists beyond just making money. Without a clear purpose, a brand is like a ship drifting aimlessly in the ocean, hoping to land somewhere interesting. Purpose gives direction, inspires action, and connects with people on a deeper level.

Think of your brand's purpose as the story you want to tell the world. It should resonate with your audience and make them feel like they're part of something bigger. Purpose is what transforms a faceless company into a brand people care about. Whether it's solving a specific problem, championing a cause, or simply making life better in some way, your purpose is the guiding light that shapes everything your brand does.

Authenticity: The Secret Sauce

People can smell fake a mile away. In a world overflowing with marketing buzzwords and polished facades, authenticity is a breath of fresh air. Exceptional brands are unapologetically themselves. They know who they are, what they stand for, and they stick to it.

Being authentic doesn't mean being perfect. It means being real. It's about showing your brand's personality, quirks, and all, in a way that feels genuine. People are drawn to brands they can trust, and trust comes from authenticity. So ditch the corporate jargon, stop trying to be everything to everyone, and just be yourself. Your audience will appreciate it—and they'll stick around for the ride.

Storytelling: Capturing Hearts and Minds

Everybody loves a good story. It's how we connect, relate, and make sense of the world. Exceptional brands understand this and use storytelling to their advantage. They don't just list features or benefits—they take their audience on a journey.

Your brand's story is more than just its history or milestones. It's about the values you stand for, the challenges you've overcome, and the impact you want to create. A good story makes your brand relatable and memorable. It helps people see the human side of your business, turning customers into loyal fans who root for you.

Crafting a great story doesn't mean you need to be dramatic or overly sentimental. It just means being honest, engaging, and consistent. The best stories are the ones that make people feel something—whether it's joy, inspiration, or even nostalgia.

Visual and Verbal Identity: The First Impression That Lasts

Let's face it—looks matter. The way your brand presents itself visually and verbally is the first thing people notice, and first impressions stick. Exceptional brands have a distinct look and feel that sets them apart. Whether it's a bold logo, a unique color palette, or a memorable tagline, everything about their identity screams "this is us."

But identity isn't just about being pretty; it's about being consistent. Your visual and verbal cues should work together to tell a cohesive story about who you are. Think about how your brand sounds when it speaks—are you witty and playful, or are you serious and professional? The tone of voice you use should match your visual style, creating a seamless experience that feels authentic and recognizable.

Your brand's identity is like its personality. It's what makes people stop, take notice, and, most importantly, remember you. So don't be afraid to be bold, creative, and a little different. After all, no one remembers the wallflower at the party.

Innovation: Staying Fresh and Exciting

Being exceptional means never settling for the status quo. Exceptional brands are always evolving, finding new ways to surprise and delight their audience. They don't just follow trends—they set them.

Innovation doesn't always mean reinventing the wheel. Sometimes, it's about taking something familiar and adding a fresh twist. It could be a new way of delivering your product, a clever marketing campaign, or even a subtle improvement that makes your customers' lives easier. The key is to keep things exciting and stay one step ahead of the competition.

Exceptional brands are curious, creative, and unafraid to take risks. They embrace change and adapt to the ever-evolving needs of their audience. By staying fresh and relevant, they ensure that people keep coming back for more.

Emotional Connection: The Magic Ingredient

People don't just buy products—they buy feelings. Exceptional brands know how to tap into emotions, creating connections that go beyond transactions. When your brand makes people feel something, it becomes more than just a name or a logo—it becomes part of their lives.

Creating an emotional connection doesn't have to be complicated. It can be as simple as making someone laugh with a clever ad, sparking nostalgia with a product, or standing up for a cause that matters to your audience. The goal is to make your brand feel human, relatable, and approachable.

When people feel connected to your brand, they're more likely to stick around, tell their friends, and become loyal advocates. And that kind of loyalty is priceless.

Consistency: The Glue That Holds It All Together

Consistency might not sound glamorous, but it's what keeps exceptional brands exceptional. It's about delivering the same high-quality experience across every interaction, whether it's your website, social media, customer service, or product packaging.

Consistency builds trust. When people know what to expect from your brand, they're more likely to keep coming back. It also reinforces your identity, making it easier for people to recognize and remember you. Imagine going to your favorite coffee shop and getting a completely different vibe every time—it wouldn't feel like your favorite anymore, would it?

Being consistent doesn't mean being boring. It means staying true to your brand's core values and personality while still leaving room for creativity and evolution. It's the balance between staying grounded and staying fresh.

Building Your Pillars: A Blueprint for Success

So, how do you build these pillars of uniqueness for your own brand? Start by asking yourself the tough questions:

Purpose: Why does your brand exist? What difference do you want to make in the world?

Authenticity: Are you being true to your values, or are you trying to be something you're not?

Storytelling: What's your brand's story, and how can you share it in a way that connects with your audience?

Identity: Does your brand look and sound distinct? Are your visuals and messaging consistent across all platforms?

Innovation: How can you keep things fresh and exciting for your audience?

Emotional Connection: What feelings do you want your brand to evoke, and how can you create those moments?

Consistency: Are you delivering the same exceptional experience every time, everywhere?

> "*Building an exceptional brand isn't something you do overnight. It takes time, effort, and a willingness to take risks. But the payoff is worth it. When you create a brand that's unique, authentic, and memorable, you're not just building a business—you're building something people love.*"

What makes a brand exceptional isn't a single trait or strategy. It's the combination of purpose, authenticity, storytelling, identity, innovation, emotional connection, and consistency that sets it apart. These pillars work together to create a brand that's not only different but also meaningful, inspiring, and unforgettable.

Exceptional brands don't happen by accident—they're built with intention and care. So, whether you're just starting out or looking to reinvent your brand, focus on these pillars. Lean into what makes you unique, embrace your quirks, and show the world who you really are. Because when you build a brand that stands tall on the pillars of uniqueness, you're not just in the game—you're changing it.

Emotional Connection and Brand Loyalty

Ever wondered why you keep choosing one brand over another, even when both offer similar products or services? It's not always about quality, price, or convenience—it's about the way a brand makes you feel. Emotional connection is the secret that transforms casual customers into die-hard loyalists. When a brand resonates with people on a deeper, emotional level, it becomes more than just a name or a logo—it becomes a part of their identity.

Let's explore the magic of emotional connection and how it fosters unshakable brand loyalty.

What is Emotional Connection?

An emotional connection happens when a brand makes customers feel understood, valued, and inspired. It goes beyond transactions; it's about creating a bond that taps into the feelings, values, and experiences of your audience.

Think about the brands you love. Whether they make you feel empowered, nostalgic, joyful, or even comforted, those emotions play a huge role in why you keep going back to them. Emotional connection is the difference between buying something because you need it and choosing something because you love it.

Why Emotional Connection Matters?

1. It Builds Trust

Trust is the foundation of any strong relationship, and emotional connection creates trust by showing customers that a brand truly understands them. When people feel that a brand "gets" them, they're more likely to believe in its promises and stick around.

2. It Drives Loyalty

Emotional bonds create loyal customers who come back time and again—not because they have to, but because they want to. These customers are less likely to switch to competitors, even if the competition offers lower prices or similar features.

3. It Encourages Advocacy

People love talking about the brands they feel connected to. When a brand strikes an emotional chord, customers become advocates, sharing their experiences with friends, family, and social media followers. This word-of-mouth marketing is priceless.

4. It Justifies Premium Pricing

Brands with strong emotional connections can charge more for their products or services. Customers are often willing to pay a premium for a brand they feel connected to because the relationship is about more than just the product—it's about the experience and the meaning behind it.

How Emotional Connection Fosters Brand Loyalty?

Storytelling is one of the most powerful tools for creating emotional connections that drive brand loyalty. Great brands tell stories that resonate deeply with their audience—stories of perseverance, humor, or shared values. When people see their own lives reflected in a brand's narrative, they naturally feel more connected to it. A compelling story isn't just about the product; it's about the feelings and experiences that surround it, turning a simple transaction into an emotional journey.

Another key driver of emotional connection is shared values and purpose. Customers want to support brands that stand for something meaningful, whether it's sustainability, social justice, or innovation. When a brand aligns with their beliefs, it creates a personal bond that goes beyond the product itself. This alignment fosters loyalty by making customers feel like they're part of a larger movement or mission.

Consistency also plays a critical role in building emotional bonds. Nothing kills loyalty faster than inconsistency. Customers expect a seamless and reliable experience every time they interact with a brand—whether it's through a website, social media, or in-store. When a brand consistently delivers on its promises, it reinforces trust and strengthens the emotional connection.

Personalization is another powerful way to nurture emotional loyalty. When customers feel seen and appreciated as individuals, it deepens their attachment to a brand. Tailored emails, birthday discounts, or thoughtful customer service interactions make customers feel valued, showing them that they are more than just a number. This personal touch creates a sense of belonging and strengthens their loyalty.

Finally, the element of surprise and delight can amplify emotional connections. Small, unexpected gestures, like a thank-you note, a free gift, or a fun surprise, can leave a lasting impression. It's not about extravagant spending—it's about making customers feel appreciated and special. These moments of delight can turn an ordinary experience into something memorable, solidifying the bond between the brand and its customers.

By leveraging storytelling, shared values, consistency, personalization, and surprise, brands can foster emotional connections that transform casual customers into loyal advocates. These emotional ties are the foundation of long-term loyalty, driving engagement, repeat business, and lasting relationships.

> "*An emotional connection is the holy grail of branding. It's the intangible force that turns casual customers into loyal advocates who stick with your brand through thick and thin. By tapping into emotions, understanding your audience, and staying authentic, you can create bonds that go beyond transactions and inspire unwavering loyalty.*
>
> *So, the next time you think about your brand strategy, remember: people don't just buy products—they buy feelings, stories, and experiences. Make those moments count, and you'll build a brand that stands the test of time.*"

Examples of Standout Brands Across Industries

Standout brands don't just survive in their industries—they redefine them. These are the brands that innovate, inspire, and resonate deeply with their audiences. They're not just providers of products or services; they're creators of experiences, movements, and identities.

1. Technology: **Apple**

Apple isn't just a tech company; it's a symbol of innovation, design excellence, and user-centric thinking. What sets Apple apart is its ability to marry cutting-edge technology with simplicity and aesthetics. From the iconic iPhone to the seamless ecosystem of devices, Apple delivers products that are not only functional but also aspirational. Its minimalistic design language, coupled with powerful storytelling in campaigns like "Think Different," has positioned it as a brand synonymous with creativity and individuality.

2. E-commerce: **Amazon**

Amazon redefined how the world shops. Its obsession with customer experience—evident in features like one-click ordering, personalized recommendations, and fast delivery—has made it the go-to platform for convenience and reliability. Amazon's standout factor lies in its relentless pursuit of innovation, from introducing the Kindle to revolutionizing cloud computing with AWS. Its commitment to customer satisfaction and adaptability to changing market demands solidifies its position as a leader in e-commerce.

3. Automotive: **Tesla**

Tesla isn't just an electric car company—it's a movement toward sustainable energy. By combining sleek design, cutting-edge technology, and environmental consciousness, Tesla has become a symbol of innovation and aspiration in the automotive industry. Its direct-to-consumer model, over-the-air software updates, and charismatic leadership have created a cult-like following. Tesla's ability to blend sustainability with luxury has redefined what it means to drive an electric vehicle.

4. Food and Beverage: **Coca-Cola**

Coca-Cola is one of the most recognizable brands in the world, and for good reason. Its ability to create emotional connections through marketing is unparalleled. Campaigns like "Share a Coke" and holiday ads featuring the Coca-Cola polar bears have made it a brand associated with happiness, togetherness, and nostalgia. Coca-Cola's global consistency in taste, packaging, and branding ensures it remains a timeless icon in the beverage industry.

5. Fashion: **Nike**

Nike's brand goes far beyond athletic apparel. It's a symbol of empowerment, perseverance, and victory. Its tagline, "Just Do It," resonates universally, inspiring people to push their limits. Nike has mastered the art of storytelling, collaborating with athletes and leveraging their stories of triumph to build an emotional connection with consumers. By combining innovative products with powerful messaging, Nike remains a leader in the highly competitive fashion and sportswear industry.

6. Hospitality: **Airbnb**

Airbnb revolutionized the hospitality industry by transforming how people travel and experience destinations. Its "Belong Anywhere" ethos speaks to a desire for authentic and personalized travel experiences. By connecting travelers with unique accommodations and local hosts, Airbnb created a sense of community and adventure. The brand's user-friendly platform and emphasis on storytelling—through hosts' and guests' experiences—set it apart from traditional hotels.

7. Beauty: **Glossier**

Glossier disrupted the beauty industry by focusing on community and authenticity. Unlike traditional beauty brands that prioritized perfection, Glossier embraced real, relatable beauty with its tagline, "Skin first. Makeup second." The brand leveraged social media and user-generated content to build a loyal community of fans. By emphasizing minimalist aesthetics and inclusive products, Glossier created a movement that resonated with millennials and Gen Z.

8. Entertainment: **Netflix**

Netflix didn't just adapt to change—it led it. From its beginnings as a DVD rental service to becoming the global leader in streaming, Netflix has consistently stayed ahead of the curve. Its commitment to producing high-quality original content, like "Stranger Things" and "The Crown," has solidified its position as a cultural powerhouse. Netflix's data-driven approach to understanding viewer preferences ensures it remains at the forefront of entertainment innovation.

9. Retail: **IKEA**

IKEA stands out in the retail space by offering affordable, stylish, and functional furniture for the masses. Its flat-pack furniture concept revolutionized how people shop for and assemble their homes. IKEA's in-store experience, complete with room displays, cafes, and kid-friendly areas, makes visiting their stores an event in itself. The brand's ability to combine practicality with Scandinavian design sensibilities has made it a global icon.

10. Education: **Duolingo**

Duolingo turned language learning into a fun and addictive game. Its free, gamified app has made learning accessible to millions worldwide. The quirky personality of its mascot, Duo, and the brand's playful tone create an engaging user experience. By blending education with entertainment, Duolingo has made itself synonymous with learning languages in the digital age.

What Makes These Brands Stand Out?

- **Customer-Centric Approach:** They put the customer's needs and experiences at the heart of everything they do.
- **Innovation:** They don't just follow trends; they set them, constantly pushing boundaries.
- **Emotional Connection:** They inspire loyalty by creating meaningful relationships with their audience.
- **Consistency:** They deliver a seamless and recognizable experience across all touchpoints.
- **Authenticity:** They stay true to their core values and mission, earning trust and admiration.

These standout brands prove that success isn't just about selling products or services—it's about creating a brand that people love, trust, and want to be a part of. Whether you're in technology, beauty, or any other industry, the principles behind these brands' success are universal and can serve as inspiration for building your own exceptional brand.

The Core Elements of Differentiation

CHAPTER FOUR

Discovering Your Brand's Core Identity

Defining Your Mission, Vision, and Values

Your brand's core identity is its essence—the DNA that defines who you are, what you stand for, and why you exist. Without it, your brand risks becoming just another face in the crowd, blending into a sea of competitors. Discovering your core identity is about getting to the heart of your brand's purpose and aligning everything you do with that foundation. At the core of this identity lie three crucial elements: your mission, vision, and values. Together, they provide clarity, direction, and authenticity that resonate with your audience.

What is Your Brand's Mission?

Your mission is the "why" behind your brand. It's the reason you exist, the problem you're solving, or the value you're adding to the world. A strong mission statement answers this question: What impact do we want to make, and for whom?

A mission isn't about lofty language or corporate jargon—it's about clarity and purpose. It should reflect your brand's unique role in the lives of your customers and inspire both your team and your audience.

For instance, if your brand creates eco-friendly products, your mission might center on sustainability and reducing environmental harm. If you're in the education space, it could focus on empowering people to learn and grow. The key is to make your mission meaningful and actionable, something that informs every decision and action your brand takes.

What is Your Brand's Vision?

If the mission is your brand's purpose, the vision is its destination. It's the "where" you're headed—the big-picture goal you're striving to achieve. While the mission focuses on the present, the vision is about the future.

Your vision should be ambitious but attainable, painting a clear picture of the impact your brand hopes to create in the long run. It's not just about what you'll achieve as a company but also the difference you'll make in your industry or community. A compelling vision statement provides direction for your brand's journey and inspires people to join you on that path.

For example, a fitness brand's vision might be to create a world where everyone has access to healthy living, while a technology company's vision could be to revolutionize the way people connect. Whatever your vision, it should be aspirational, memorable, and aligned with your mission.

What Are Your Brand's Values?

Your values are the guiding principles that shape your brand's behavior and decisions. They define how you operate, interact with customers, and contribute to the world. While the mission is about your purpose and the vision about your future, the values are about how you get there.

Strong values are authentic and specific—not generic buzzwords. They reflect your brand's personality and set the standard for how you operate internally and externally. For example, if one of your values is "innovation," it should influence everything from product development to marketing strategies. If "transparency" is a core value, it should be evident in how you communicate with your audience.

Values are what make your brand relatable and trustworthy. They create an emotional connection with your audience and foster loyalty by showing what you stand for.

How to Define Your Mission, Vision, and Values

1. Reflect on Your Purpose

Start by asking, Why does my brand exist? What problem am I solving? Who am I helping? These questions will help you define your mission. Be specific and focus on the real-world impact you want to make.

2. Imagine Your Ideal Future

Think about where you want your brand to be in 5, 10, or 20 years. What change do you want to create in your industry or community? Your vision should be ambitious yet achievable—a statement that motivates your team and inspires your audience.

3. Identify Your Core Beliefs

Reflect on what principles guide your decision-making. What do you value most as a brand? Authenticity? Sustainability? Creativity? Your values should be the foundation of how you operate and interact with the world.

4. Make it Concise and Clear

Your mission, vision, and values should be easy to understand and remember. Avoid jargon or overly complex language. These statements are not just for internal use—they're the foundation of how you communicate with your audience.

5. Involve Your Team

Your brand identity is a shared effort. Involve your team in the process to ensure that your mission, vision, and values resonate with everyone. Their insights can provide valuable perspectives and help you create something truly authentic.

6. Test and Refine

Once you've drafted your mission, vision, and values, test them. Do they resonate with your target audience? Do they feel authentic to your brand? Refine them as needed to ensure they reflect your core identity.

Why Your Mission, Vision, and Values Matter?

Defining your mission, vision, and values isn't just a checkbox exercise for branding—it's the strategic foundation upon which your entire business operates. These elements provide clear direction, acting as a compass for decision-making. When every action aligns with your brand's purpose and goals, it creates consistency and focus, ensuring that your efforts contribute to the bigger picture. They also inspire loyalty among customers, who are naturally drawn to brands with a clear sense of purpose and strong values. When people see what you stand for and believe in, it builds trust and fosters a deeper emotional connection, turning one-time buyers into lifelong advocates.

A compelling mission and vision also serve as a powerful motivator for your team. Employees who understand and resonate with your brand's purpose feel a sense of pride and alignment in their work, which enhances engagement and productivity. Beyond internal benefits, your mission, vision, and values differentiate your brand in a crowded marketplace. In a world where countless businesses compete for attention, these core elements set you apart, showing customers why you're not just another option but the right choice. When clearly defined and authentically communicated, your mission, vision, and values become the heartbeat of your brand, driving growth, connection, and long-term success.

> *"Discovering your brand's core identity is about understanding who you are, what you stand for, and where you're going. Your mission, vision, and values are more than words—they're the heart of your brand, shaping every decision, interaction, and strategy.*
>
> *When you define these elements with clarity and authenticity, you're not just building a brand—you're building a legacy. So take the time to reflect, refine, and articulate your core identity. Because a brand with a clear mission, a compelling vision, and strong values isn't just*

memorable—it's unstoppable."

The Role of Storytelling in Branding

In a world where attention spans are shrinking and markets are overflowing with choices, storytelling has become an essential tool for brands to stand out and connect with their audiences. A good story does more than just describe a product or service—it captures attention, evokes emotions, and leaves a lasting impression. People are naturally drawn to stories because they resonate on a human level. Brands that embrace storytelling aren't just selling something; they're creating experiences, forging connections, and building loyalty.

Why Storytelling Matters in Branding

In today's noisy, fast-paced world, a well-crafted story has the power to grab attention in ways that statistics or generic advertisements simply cannot. With countless marketing messages vying for people's focus, a compelling narrative stands out as the hook that makes them stop scrolling, lean in, and listen. Storytelling captures attention by engaging the human desire for connection and intrigue, keeping audiences engaged far beyond the superficial level of traditional advertising.

More importantly, stories evoke emotional connections, which are the foundation of memorable branding. Whether a story sparks joy, nostalgia, inspiration, or empathy, emotions create a lasting impact. A good story doesn't just explain what a brand does—it makes people feel something. These feelings not only make a brand memorable but also drive loyalty and action, creating a deeper bond with customers.

For brands with complex or innovative offerings, storytelling serves as a powerful tool to simplify ideas. It frames products or services within relatable, human contexts, making them more approachable and easier to understand. Instead of overwhelming audiences with technical jargon, a well-told story demonstrates how a brand fits into their lives, solving problems or enhancing experiences in meaningful ways.

Storytelling also builds authenticity and trust, two of the most critical elements in modern branding. By sharing stories about origins, challenges, or values, a brand reveals its human side and demonstrates transparency. This authenticity fosters trust because it shows that the brand isn't just a faceless entity but one that customers can relate to and believe in.

Finally, storytelling creates differentiation by giving a brand a unique voice and identity. Every brand has a story, but the way it's told sets it apart from competitors. In an industry where many brands rely on generic messaging, a compelling story becomes a signature, something that competitors cannot replicate. This uniqueness makes the brand stand out and leaves a lasting impression, making storytelling an indispensable element of successful branding.

How to Incorporate Storytelling into Your Branding?

1. Start with Your "Why"

Every great story starts with a purpose. Why does your brand exist? What motivated its creation? Sharing the "why" behind your brand humanizes it and makes it relatable.

2. Define Your Brand Character

Think of your brand as a character in a story. Is it bold and adventurous? Warm and nurturing? Defining your brand's personality helps shape the tone and style of your storytelling.

3. Highlight Real People and Experiences

Stories about real people—your customers, employees, or founders—add authenticity and emotional depth. Sharing testimonials, user-generated content, or behind-the-scenes glimpses makes your brand feel alive and relatable.

4. Use a Consistent Narrative Across Channels

Your story should be cohesive and consistent, whether it's shared on your website, social media, or advertising campaigns. A fragmented or contradictory story can confuse your audience and weaken your brand's impact.

5. Show, Don't Just Tell

Great storytelling is about creating experiences, not just delivering information. Use visuals, videos, and interactive elements to bring your story to life and immerse your audience in your brand's narrative.

Examples of Storytelling in Action

- ***Origin Stories***

Sharing how your brand was born adds authenticity and relatability. It shows your audience that your brand started with a purpose, a dream, or a desire to solve a problem.

- ***Customer Stories***

Highlighting the experiences of your customers demonstrates the real-world impact of your brand. These stories show that you're not just selling a product; you're improving lives.

- ***Social and Cultural Relevance***

Weaving your brand into the fabric of current events or cultural moments can make it feel timely and relevant. A good example is using storytelling to support causes or social issues that align with your values.

> "***The Long-Term Impact of Storytelling in Branding***
>
> *Storytelling is more than just a marketing tactic—it's a strategy for building long-term relationships. A great story creates a sense of familiarity, making your brand feel like an old friend rather than a faceless corporation. Over time, this bond fosters trust, loyalty, and advocacy.*

> *When done well, storytelling doesn't just attract customers; it turns them into fans who are emotionally invested in your brand. They'll remember your story, share it with others, and keep coming back because they feel connected to who you are, not just what you sell.*"

The role of storytelling in branding cannot be overstated. It's the bridge between your brand and your audience, turning transactions into relationships and customers into advocates. A well-told story has the power to captivate, inspire, and create a lasting impact. So, if your brand isn't telling a story yet, it's time to start. Find your narrative, share it authentically, and watch as it transforms your brand into something people love, trust, and remember.

CHAPTER FIVE

DIFFERENTIATION STRATEGIES

How to Identify and Leverage Your Unique Selling Proposition (USP)

Imagine you're at a talent show where everyone is juggling the same three flaming torches. It's cool at first, but soon the crowd is bored. Then, you step on stage and juggle chainsaws while reciting Shakespeare. Suddenly, all eyes are on you. That's the magic of a Unique Selling Proposition (USP)—it's the thing that makes you so captivating, people can't help but choose you. In the crowded marketplace, your USP is what makes your brand unforgettable, irresistible, and downright magnetic.

But how do you find your USP? And once you've nailed it, how do you show it off in a way that gets everyone talking?

What is a USP, and Why Should You Care?

Your USP is your brand's superpower. It's the one thing you do better, smarter, or cooler than anyone else. It's not about being loud; it's about being different in a way that matters. Your USP tells the world, "Here's why you need me in your life," and gives people a reason to care. Without it, you're just juggling the same old torches.

How to Discover Your USP (Without Losing Your Mind)

1. Get Inside Your Customers' Heads

First, you've got to know who you're talking to. What do your customers dream about, worry about, or desperately want? What keeps them up at night, and how can your brand make their lives easier or better? Your USP starts where their needs meet your strengths.

Pro Tip: Spend some time lurking where your customers hang out—social media, review sites, or forums. (But don't be creepy. Nobody likes a weird lurker.)

2. Spy on Your Competition

You're not here to copy your competitors—you're here to outshine them. What are they doing well? More importantly, where are they falling flat? Finding the gaps in their offerings is like discovering a secret doorway to success.

Pro Tip: Make a list of competitors and analyze what they claim as their "thing." Then figure out how your brand can do it differently—or better.

3. Own What Makes You Special

Maybe you're lightning-fast, obsessively eco-friendly, or the only brand that makes socks with built-in USB chargers (okay, weird, but you get the idea). Your USP isn't just about being different; it's about being uniquely valuable.

Pro Tip: Ask yourself, "If my brand disappeared tomorrow, what would people miss the most?"

4. Solve a Problem Like a Boss

The best USPs solve a real problem. Customers don't just buy products—they buy solutions. If your brand makes their lives easier, more exciting, or just plain better, that's your ticket to stand out.

Pro Tip: Frame your USP as the answer to your customers' biggest "pain point." Think, "We're the aspirin for your headache."

5. Add a Dash of Personality

A killer USP is more than just facts and figures—it's about how you make people feel. Think about the vibe your brand gives off. Are you fun and quirky, or sleek and sophisticated? Your personality is part of your USP, so let it shine.

Pro Tip: Write your USP as if you were explaining it to a friend over coffee (or cocktails). Keep it real.

How to Flaunt Your USP Like a Rockstar

Your Unique Selling Proposition (USP) should be at the core of everything you do—it's the anthem your brand lives by. Incorporate it into your tagline, advertisements, website, and even your email sign-offs. Think of it as your rallying cry that boldly communicates what makes you unique. Instead of saying something generic like, "We sell shoes," transform it into something inspiring like, "We help people run faster, jump higher, and dance like no one's watching." Your USP isn't just a statement; it's your brand's identity, so make it loud and proud.

But a USP is only as good as your ability to deliver on it. A promise that isn't kept is just empty words. If your USP is all about speed, ensure you're the fastest in the game. If it's about quality, aim for perfection every time. Consistency is key here. Leverage customer feedback to continuously evaluate how well you're living up to your USP, and make adjustments as needed to ensure it remains more than just talk.

To truly bring your USP to life, tell stories that showcase its impact. People don't remember a list of features or facts—they remember compelling narratives. Share testimonials, case studies, or your brand's origin story to illustrate how your USP has made a tangible difference. Think of your USP as the star of a movie and ensure it gets plenty of screen time. Whether it's a customer sharing how your product transformed their day or a behind-the-scenes glimpse of your innovative process, stories make your USP relatable and memorable.

Visuals are another powerful way to flaunt your USP. It's not just about words; it's about creating an experience. Use bold colors, eye-catching videos, and design elements that reflect your unique value. For instance, if your brand is fun and quirky, your visuals should scream fun and quirky. A thoughtfully designed logo or tagline that encapsulates the essence of your USP in one glance can leave a lasting impression and make your brand instantly recognizable.

Finally, keep your USP fresh and relevant. Markets evolve, and so do customer needs, so it's essential to revisit your USP regularly to ensure it's still aligned with your audience. Treat it like a playlist that needs updating to stay exciting and in tune. Set a reminder every six months to evaluate whether your USP still resonates and excites, and be prepared to refine it if necessary.

> *"When you consistently communicate, deliver, and evolve your USP, you elevate it from a statement to a powerful driver of your brand's success. By turning it into your anthem, keeping it alive in your storytelling, and ensuring it reflects your brand's visual and emotional identity, you'll make your USP the centerpiece of a brand people can't help but notice—and love."*

The Biggest USP Mistakes (and How to Avoid Them)

Crafting a strong Unique Selling Proposition (USP) is essential for differentiating your brand, but even the best intentions can go awry if common mistakes creep in. A weak or poorly thought-out USP can confuse customers, erode trust, and leave your brand blending in with the competition. Let's take a closer look at the biggest USP pitfalls and how you can steer clear of them.

- **Being Generic**

Saying, "We sell great products" or "We provide excellent service" isn't a USP—it's a default statement that could apply to virtually any business. A generic USP is bland, forgettable, and offers no real reason for customers to choose you over someone else. Your USP needs to highlight what makes your brand truly unique and valuable.

A great USP is specific, memorable, and meaningful. Instead of saying, "We sell quality shoes," you could say, "We make shoes so comfortable, it feels like walking on clouds." The difference is night and day—one is generic and uninspiring, while the other is visual and emotionally engaging. Specificity grabs attention and helps people remember your brand long after they've encountered it.

How to Avoid This Mistake: Dive deep into what sets your brand apart. Focus on a specific feature, benefit, or value that only your brand provides. Be bold in communicating it, and avoid buzzwords that sound impressive but mean little.

- **Overpromising**

It's tempting to go big when crafting your USP, but there's a fine line between boldness and overpromising. If you claim to be "the fastest delivery service in the world" or promise "life-changing results overnight," you're setting expectations that may be impossible to meet. The problem with overpromising is that failing to deliver on these inflated claims damages your credibility and erodes trust.

A USP should set you apart, but it also needs to be grounded in reality. Customers are drawn to brands they can rely on, and trust is earned through consistency and honesty. Overpromising might get attention initially, but the long-term damage from unmet expectations far outweighs any short-term gains.

How to Avoid This Mistake: Be ambitious but realistic. Make sure your USP reflects something you can consistently deliver. If speed is your USP, ensure your processes can support quick turnarounds. If quality is your focus, invest in systems that guarantee excellence every time. Underpromise and overdeliver to build lasting trust and loyalty.

- **Trying to Be Everything to Everyone**

One of the most common USP mistakes is trying to cover all the bases. You might want to be the fastest, cheapest, most luxurious, and most sustainable brand all at once, but here's the truth: you can't be everything to everyone. Trying to do so dilutes your message, confuses your audience, and makes it difficult for your brand to stand out.

When your USP lacks focus, it becomes hard for customers to understand what makes you different. Instead of being remembered as the go-to for one thing, you risk being seen as just another option in the crowd. A strong USP is clear, focused, and aligned with what matters most to your target audience.

How to Avoid This Mistake: Choose a lane and own it. Decide what you want to be known for and build your brand around that. If your strength is affordability, lean into it. If you're focused on luxury, make that your defining trait. By narrowing your focus, you can craft a USP that resonates deeply with the right audience and establishes your brand as a leader in its niche.

Your USP isn't just what makes your brand different—it's what makes it better. It's your secret recipe ingredient, your mic drop, your standing ovation moment. By discovering what makes your brand unique and flaunting it with confidence, you'll stand out, win hearts, and keep your audience coming back for more.

So go ahead—juggle the chainsaws, recite the Shakespeare, and show the world why your brand is the one they can't live without. Because when you own your USP, you don't just compete—you shine.

The Power of Niche Markets

In a world where big brands dominate the mainstream, trying to appeal to everyone can often mean appealing to no one. This is where the power of niche markets comes into play. Niche markets allow brands to focus their efforts on a specific audience with unique needs, desires, or preferences. By tailoring your products, services, and messaging to a smaller, more defined group, you can stand out, build loyalty, and establish yourself as the go-to solution for that audience. In short, when you own your niche, you create opportunities for growth, even in the most competitive industries.

What is a Niche Market?

A niche market is a smaller segment of a larger market defined by unique characteristics, preferences, or unmet needs. Instead of targeting the entire population, you focus on a specific group—whether it's vegan athletes, eco-conscious travelers, or luxury pet owners. Niche markets aren't just about demographics like age or income; they can also be based on lifestyle, values, or even quirky hobbies. The beauty of a niche market is that it allows you to focus on quality over quantity, building deeper connections with a smaller, highly engaged audience.

Why Niche Markets Are Powerful?

Imagine trying to stand out in a crowd of a million people all shouting the same thing. Tough, right? Now picture a room with just 50 people, all looking for someone who can do exactly what you do. That's the magic of a niche market. In a niche, the competition isn't deafening, and it's much easier to get noticed. By zeroing in on a specific audience, you can tailor your offerings to fit their unique needs perfectly, making your brand the one they think of first—and possibly the only one they need.

But the magic doesn't stop there. Niche audiences are like loyal fans who've been waiting for someone to finally cater to them. They often feel ignored by the big, mainstream brands, so when you show up with something that feels like it was made just for them, they're hooked. These customers aren't just buyers—they're believers. The connection is real, and loyalty comes naturally because you've shown that you truly get them.

Another perk? You can charge more for your niche products or services because exclusivity has its value. When people feel like something is tailor-made for their specific needs or desires, they're happy to pay a premium. It's like the difference between buying a mass-produced t-shirt and getting a custom-made one that fits like a dream—one feels ordinary, and the other feels special.

Marketing also becomes a breeze. Instead of trying to shout louder than everyone else in a crowded market, you get to whisper directly to the people who are already interested in what you have to offer. Your campaigns can be hyper-focused, hitting all the right notes with your audience. It's not just efficient—it's downright satisfying to see your message resonate deeply with the people it's meant for.

And let's not forget the playground of possibilities. Niche markets are often unexplored territory, leaving you room to innovate, experiment, and create something no one else has thought of yet. You're not just filling a gap—you're shaping the market for your audience. Whether it's solving a pain point they've always had or surprising them with a product they didn't even know they needed, the opportunities to wow them are endless.

> "*So, why are niche markets powerful? Because they're your chance to stand out, connect deeply, and thrive in a way that's uniquely yours. When you find your niche, you're not just another voice in the crowd—you're the one they've been waiting for.*"

How to Find and Dominate a Niche Market?

1. Identify Gaps in the Market

Start by analyzing your industry to spot underserved groups or unmet needs. These gaps represent opportunities to create value and establish your brand in a specific niche.

Example: If the fitness industry focuses heavily on young athletes, you might find an opportunity to serve older adults looking for low-impact exercise solutions.

2. Understand Your Audience Deeply

Knowing your niche audience inside and out is crucial. What are their pain points? What motivates them? What do they value most? The more you understand their needs, the better you can tailor your offerings and messaging to resonate with them.

3. Develop Tailored Solutions

Once you've identified your niche, design products or services that solve their specific problems. Focus on creating solutions that feel like they were made just for them.

Example: A skincare brand might develop a line specifically for people with sensitive, allergy-prone skin, using hypoallergenic and fragrance-free ingredients.

4. Position Yourself as the Expert

In a niche market, being recognized as the go-to expert can set you apart. Share valuable insights, create educational content, and engage with your audience in meaningful ways to build authority and trust.

5. Use Targeted Marketing

Customize your marketing efforts to speak directly to your niche. Whether it's through social media platforms, email campaigns, or niche-specific forums, your message should feel personal and relevant to your audience.

6. Foster a Community

Niche audiences thrive on connection. Create opportunities for your customers to engage with your brand and with each other. Building a community around your niche strengthens loyalty and helps spread word-of-mouth recommendations.

Challenges of Niche Markets and How to Overcome Them

Niche markets are like hidden treasure chests—filled with unique opportunities but not without their share of challenges. One of the biggest hurdles is the smaller audience size. While having a focused group of loyal customers is great, it can also mean your growth feels a bit like trying to fill a swimming pool with a teaspoon. The key to overcoming this? Deliver exceptional value. When your product or service feels like the perfect solution to your niche audience's needs, they'll not only stick around—they'll shout your praises from the rooftops (or at least post about you on social media). Word-of-mouth becomes your secret weapon, turning loyal customers into your unofficial brand ambassadors.

But wait, there's more! Staying relevant in a niche market is another challenge that requires constant attention. People's needs and preferences aren't static; they evolve, sometimes faster than you'd expect. What's a must-have today could be "meh" tomorrow. That's why it's crucial to keep your finger on the pulse of your audience. Think of it as an ongoing conversation—listen to their feedback, follow the trends that matter to them, and don't be afraid to pivot or tweak your offerings. Staying one step ahead of your niche ensures your brand remains their go-to choice, even as the market shifts.

Niche markets require creativity and resilience. You won't have the massive audience or budgets of mainstream players, but that's part of the charm. With a smaller, more engaged audience, you can experiment, take risks, and build stronger relationships. Sure, the road might be a little bumpier, but the rewards—deep loyalty, genuine connections, and a space you can truly own—are worth it. Think of your niche market as a tight-knit community that thrives on your authenticity and dedication. Stay innovative, keep delivering value, and let your passion shine. With these strategies, you can overcome the challenges and turn your niche into your brand's sweet spot.

The power of niche markets lies in their ability to help brands focus, differentiate, and connect on a deeper level with their audience. By finding and serving a specific group, you can carve out a unique space in the market where your brand is not just another option—it's the option. Embracing a niche strategy allows you to become a specialist, innovate creatively, and foster loyalty that drives long-term success. So, instead of trying to appeal to the masses, zero in on your niche, own it, and watch your brand thrive.

CHAPTER SIX

The Visual and Verbal Identity

Designing a Distinctive Logo, Color Palette, and Typography

Your brand's visual and verbal identity is like its outfit and voice—it's what people see and hear first, and it leaves a lasting impression. A well-crafted identity is the secret sauce that makes your brand instantly recognizable and memorable. Think of it as the personality of your business, expressed through design elements like your logo, color palette, and typography, paired with the tone of your messaging. When done right, your visual and verbal identity works together to tell your brand's story at a glance. Let's break down how to design these elements to stand out in a crowded marketplace.

Designing a Distinctive Logo -- Your logo is the face of your brand—its essence distilled into a single symbol. A great logo is more than just visually appealing; it's meaningful, versatile, and unique. It should capture the spirit of your brand while being simple enough to be recognized at a glance.

When designing a logo, focus on clarity and scalability. Your logo should look just as good on a billboard as it does on a business card. Avoid overly complex designs or trendy elements that might feel outdated in a few years. Instead, aim for timelessness—a logo that can grow with your brand. Whether it's a bold icon, a sleek wordmark, or a combination of the two, ensure your logo is aligned with your brand's personality and mission.

Choosing a Standout Color Palette-- Color is one of the most powerful tools in your branding arsenal. It evokes emotions, communicates your brand's tone, and makes you instantly recognizable. A well-thought-out color palette can make your brand pop, but choosing the right colors is about more than just aesthetics—it's about psychology.

For example, blue often conveys trust and reliability, making it popular in industries like tech and finance. Red signals energy and passion, while green is associated with growth and sustainability. Choose colors that align with the emotions and values you want your brand to convey. Aim for a primary color that anchors your identity, supported by complementary colors for versatility. And don't forget about contrast—your colors should work well together while remaining visually striking.

Crafting Typography That Speaks Volumes -- Typography is often overlooked, but it's a cornerstone of a strong visual identity. The fonts you choose convey a lot about your brand's character. Is your brand playful and creative? Go for quirky, hand-drawn fonts. Is it sleek and modern? Opt for clean, sans-serif typefaces. Typography should enhance your brand's message, not overshadow it.

Choose one or two primary fonts that you'll use consistently across all touchpoints. This includes your website, social media, print materials, and packaging. Pair a display font for headlines with a legible body font for longer text. Consistency in typography creates cohesion and makes your brand instantly recognizable.

Combining Visual and Verbal for a Cohesive Identity

Your visual elements—logo, colors, and typography—should work seamlessly with your verbal identity. Your tone of voice should reflect your visuals and vice versa. For example, if your color palette is bold and energetic, your messaging should be dynamic and engaging. If your visuals are minimalist and clean, your tone might be calm and sophisticated.

Your verbal identity includes your brand's tagline, messaging, and the way you communicate with your audience. Are you playful and witty, or professional and authoritative? This tone should be consistent across all platforms, from your website copy to your social media posts.

Tips for Building a Memorable Visual and Verbal Identity

Keep It Simple: Simplicity makes your brand easier to remember. Don't clutter your logo or overwhelm your palette with too many colors.

Be Consistent: Use the same colors, fonts, and tone across all touchpoints. Consistency builds trust and recognition.

Stay True to Your Brand: Your identity should reflect your brand's mission, vision, and values. Authenticity is key.

Test It Out: Show your designs to others for feedback. Does your logo look good in different sizes? Do your colors evoke the right emotions? Does your tone resonate?

Think Long-Term: Your identity should evolve with your brand but remain relevant over time. Avoid overly trendy designs that might feel outdated too quickly.

Your visual and verbal identity is more than just how your brand looks and sounds—it's how it makes people feel. A distinctive logo, cohesive color palette, and thoughtful typography combine to create a brand that's not only recognizable but also emotionally engaging. Paired with a consistent and authentic tone of voice, your identity becomes a powerful tool for building connections, fostering loyalty, and standing out in a crowded market. Remember, your identity isn't just a reflection of your brand—it's an invitation for your audience to connect with who you are and what you stand for.

Crafting a Memorable Tagline and Voice

Your tagline and voice are like your brand's calling card—they're the words that stick in people's minds long after they've interacted with you. A great tagline can distill the essence of your brand into a few memorable words, while your voice gives those words personality and character. Together, they create a lasting impression that resonates with your audience and builds emotional connections. Let's explore how to craft a tagline and voice that make your brand unforgettable.

The Art of Crafting a Memorable Tagline

A tagline is more than a catchy phrase—it's your brand's promise in a nutshell. It encapsulates who you are, what you do, and why you matter. A great tagline should be short, clear, and emotionally resonant. Think about the most iconic taglines: "Just Do It," "Because You're Worth It," or "Think Different." They don't just describe a product—they inspire action, emotion, or a sense of belonging.

To create your tagline, start by identifying the core of your brand's mission and what sets you apart. Ask yourself: What's the one thing I want people to remember about my brand? Keep it simple and avoid jargon—your audience should understand it instantly. A good rule of thumb? If it doesn't stick in your head after one read, it won't stick in theirs either.

Don't shy away from injecting some personality into your tagline. If your brand is playful, your tagline can reflect that with humor or wit. If you're more sophisticated, opt for something polished and inspiring. The goal is to leave an impression that aligns with your overall brand identity.

Finding Your Brand Voice

Your brand voice is how you communicate with your audience, and it's just as important as what you're saying. It's the personality behind your words, shaping how your brand feels to your customers. Whether you're playful, professional, quirky, or compassionate, your voice should be authentic to who you are and consistent across all platforms.

To discover your brand voice, start by considering your audience. Who are they, and how do they want to be spoken to? A tech-savvy Gen Z audience might appreciate a casual, emoji-filled tone, while a professional B2B audience may expect a more formal and authoritative voice.

Next, reflect on your brand's personality. If your brand were a person, how would they talk? Are they the friendly neighbor, the cheeky best friend, or the wise mentor? Use these traits to guide your tone.

Consistency is key. Your voice should sound the same whether it's a tweet, an email, or a tagline. Create a style guide that outlines how your brand "speaks," including preferred words, phrases, and tone, so everyone on your team stays on the same page.

How Tagline and Voice Work Together

Your tagline and voice should work in harmony to reinforce your brand identity. The tagline sets the tone—it's your brand's elevator pitch—while the voice carries that tone into every interaction. For example, a tagline like "Live Boldly" suggests a confident, adventurous voice, while "We Make It Simple" implies clarity, ease, and straightforwardness.

Things to keep in mind...

Be Authentic: Your tagline and voice should reflect your brand's true personality. Forced or inconsistent messaging can feel disingenuous.

Focus on Emotion: People connect with brands that make them feel something. Whether it's excitement, trust, or inspiration, aim to evoke an emotional response.

Test and Refine: Before finalizing your tagline or voice, test them with your audience. Does it resonate? Is it memorable? Gather feedback and tweak as needed.

Keep It Simple: The best taglines are short and sweet, while the best voices are easy to understand. Avoid overcomplicating things.

A memorable tagline and a consistent brand voice are powerful tools for leaving a lasting impression. Together, they

shape how people perceive and connect with your brand. By crafting a tagline that captures your essence and a voice that brings your personality to life, you create a cohesive identity that resonates with your audience and keeps your brand top of mind. Remember, it's not just about what you say—it's how you say it. So, find your voice, own your tagline, and start building those unforgettable connections.

Designing Exceptional Brand Experiences

CHAPTER SEVEN

FROM PRODUCT TO EXPERIENCE

Shifting Focus from Features to Customer Experience

In today's competitive market, having a great product is no longer enough. Customers don't just want to buy something; they want to feel something. This is why brands are shifting their focus from simply highlighting product features to creating memorable and immersive customer experiences. A great experience transforms a product into a story, a solution, or even a lifestyle, making it far more compelling to consumers. Let's explore why this shift is essential and how brands can make it happen.

Why Focus on Experience Over Features?

Features are important—they explain what a product does and why it's useful. But on their own, they rarely create emotional connections. Customers don't buy a camera because it has "20 megapixels" or a car because it has a "V6 engine." They buy the ability to capture breathtaking memories or the thrill of driving on the open road. Focusing solely on features risks reducing your brand to a list of specs, leaving little room for emotional engagement or loyalty.

Customer experience, on the other hand, is all about how your brand makes people feel throughout their journey with you—from the moment they discover you to long after their purchase. An exceptional experience not only satisfies functional needs but also delivers emotional and psychological value.

The Power of Experience in Driving Loyalty

When a product is tied to a great experience, it becomes more than just an object—it becomes part of the customer's identity. Think of brands that deliver seamless, enjoyable, or even delightful interactions. Customers remember those moments, and they return not just for the product but for the way it makes them feel.

A focus on experience also creates opportunities for differentiation. In a world where many products have similar features, the experience becomes the deciding factor. If two fitness trackers have identical functionality but one brand offers better onboarding, personalized insights, and engaging community features, it's clear which one will win hearts.

How to Shift from Features to Experience?

Understand the Customer Journey

Start by mapping out every touchpoint in your customer's journey, from awareness to post-purchase. Where can you add value or create moments of delight? Understanding your audience's needs and emotions at each stage is crucial.

Tell Stories Around Your Product

Instead of talking about what your product can do, show what it can achieve for your customers. Highlight how your product solves real problems or enhances lives. Use storytelling to make the experience relatable and memorable.

Personalize the Experience

Customers value brands that treat them as individuals. Use data and insights to tailor the experience—whether it's through personalized recommendations, customized packaging, or thank-you messages that feel genuine.

Design for Simplicity and Delight

Simplicity is the foundation of a great experience. Make your product intuitive and easy to use, and go the extra mile to add moments of delight. It could be a playful app interface, unexpected perks, or exceptional customer service that leaves a lasting impression.

Create Emotional Touchpoints

Think beyond functionality and focus on how your product fits into your customer's life. Does it inspire confidence, spark joy, or provide comfort? Highlight these emotional benefits in your messaging and interactions.

Involve the Customer in Your Story

Build a sense of community by involving customers in your brand's journey. Encourage reviews, user-generated content, or social media shares that celebrate their experience with your product. When customers feel like they're part of something bigger, their connection to your brand deepens.

> "***Examples of Experience-Focused Shifts***
>
> *A coffee company doesn't just sell coffee; it creates an environment where people can unwind, connect, or work productively.*
>
> *A subscription box isn't just a delivery service; it's an experience of surprise, discovery, and joy every month.*
>
> *A fitness brand doesn't just sell equipment; it builds a community that supports and motivates its users to achieve their goals.*"

Benefits of Prioritizing Experience

Imagine this: you visit a café that not only serves amazing coffee but also greets you with your favorite playlist, remembers your name, and adds a little smiley face to your latte art. You don't just leave caffeinated—you leave with a warm fuzzy feeling that keeps you coming back. That's the magic of prioritizing customer experience. By creating stronger emotional connections, you make customers feel invested in your brand, like it's their happy place. These connections transform casual buyers into loyal fans who can't help but stick around.

But the benefits don't stop there. A great experience has a ripple effect—when people love interacting with your brand, they talk about it. Whether it's a glowing review, a social media post, or an enthusiastic recommendation to a friend, word-of-mouth marketing becomes your secret weapon. And here's the cherry on top: a memorable experience makes your product feel more valuable. Customers are often willing to pay a premium because they're not just buying something—they're investing in a feeling, a moment, or a story they want to be part of. So, go ahead and create experiences worth talking (and paying) for—you won't regret it.

Shifting your focus from product features to customer experience is no longer optional—it's essential for building a brand that stands out and thrives. By prioritizing how your product fits into your customers' lives and makes them feel, you create a connection that goes far beyond functionality. People may forget a feature, but they'll never forget how your brand made them feel. So, design experiences that matter, tell stories that inspire, and watch as your brand transforms into something truly unforgettable.

The Importance of Delivering Delight at Every Touchpoint

Think about the last time a brand genuinely surprised you in the best way—maybe it was an unexpected thank-you note, lightning-fast delivery, or an extra little treat tucked into your order. Whatever it was, it likely left you with a big smile and a great story to tell. That's the power of delivering delight at every touchpoint. It's about turning ordinary interactions into extraordinary moments that make customers feel valued, appreciated, and eager to return.

Delight isn't just about going the extra mile; it's about understanding what matters most to your customers and showing them you care in meaningful ways. Whether it's a seamless website experience, a friendly and knowledgeable customer service team, or packaging that feels like opening a gift, every interaction is an opportunity to leave a lasting impression. When customers fee

l delighted at each stage of their journey, they're more likely to develop a strong emotional connection to your brand—and that connection is the foundation of loyalty.

Delivering delight also has the power to turn customers into brand advocates. People love sharing positive experiences, especially when they're unexpected. By consistently creating moments of joy, you give them stories to tell—whether it's a glowing review, a social media post, or a personal recommendation. These word-of-mouth referrals not only enhance your reputation but also attract new customers who are eager to see what the buzz is about.

But let's not forget the practical side of delight. When you focus on delivering exceptional experiences at every touchpoint, you reduce friction and build trust. Customers appreciate brands that make their lives easier, anticipate their needs, and handle challenges gracefully. Whether it's a smooth checkout process, a helpful chatbot, or clear communication about delivery updates, delighting your customers ensures they feel confident and cared for.

Ultimately, delivering delight at every touchpoint transforms your brand from "just another option" into one that people actively choose and recommend. It's the secret ingredient that makes your brand memorable, your customers loyal, and your reputation stellar. So, take every interaction as a chance to surprise, impress, and delight—because those small moments of joy are what keep your customers coming back for more.

CHAPTER EIGHT

The Role of Emotional Branding

Creating Connections Through Empathy and Authenticity

Let's face it—people don't fall in love with a brand because of its product specs or discounts. They fall in love because that brand gets them. That's the magic of emotional branding. It's about connecting with your audience on a human level, making them feel seen, heard, and valued. When you build your brand with empathy and authenticity, you're not just selling products; you're creating a relationship that feels like a warm hug.

First up, empathy. Think of it as putting yourself in your customers' shoes (or sneakers, slippers, or stilettos). What keeps them awake at night? What makes them smile? A brand that understands these emotions can speak directly to their hearts. For example, a fitness brand isn't just selling leggings—it's telling people, "You've got this, and we're here to cheer you on every step of the way!" When you tap into what your audience cares about, you create a connection that feels less like marketing and more like a meaningful conversation.

Now let's talk authenticity. Customers can spot fake vibes faster than a toddler can find candy. Authenticity means showing your brand's true personality—warts and all. Share your origin story, own your quirks, and stick to your values. If your brand is goofy, lean into it. If it's sleek and polished, let that shine. Authenticity isn't about being perfect; it's about being real. Imagine you're at a party—who's more interesting: the person telling a rehearsed pitch or the one sharing a funny story about how they accidentally brought their cat to work? Exactly. Be the cat story.

Here's the best part: when you nail emotional branding, customers don't just buy from you—they root for you. They tell their friends about you, defend you when the competition comes calling, and stick with you through thick and thin. Why? Because you're not just a brand; you're their brand.

> "*So, what's the secret? Keep it real, listen to your audience, and speak to their hearts. When you lead with empathy and authenticity, you're not just building a brand—you're building a relationship that lasts. And that, my friend, is branding gold. ?*"

Building Trust and a Lasting Impression

The Foundation of Brand Loyalty - In the world of branding, trust is your golden ticket. It's what turns first-time buyers into lifelong customers, skeptics into advocates, and competitors into mere background noise. But trust isn't something you can buy or demand—it's earned, nurtured, and, most importantly, maintained. Building trust is about consistency, authenticity, and delivering on your promises at every turn. When you combine trust with a memorable impression, you create a brand that not only stands out but also sticks around in the minds and hearts of your audience.

Why Trust Matters

Trust is the glue that holds any relationship together, including the one between a brand and its customers. Without trust, your brand is just another logo in a crowded market. People trust brands that are reliable, transparent, and aligned with their values. When trust exists, customers feel confident in choosing you—whether it's for the first time or the fiftieth. It's the foundation of loyalty, referrals, and repeat business, all of which are essential for long-term success.

But here's the catch: trust is fragile. A single misstep—like a product that doesn't meet expectations, poor customer service, or an unfulfilled promise—can break it. That's why it's crucial to prioritize trust-building as a core part of your branding strategy.

How to Build Trust Through Authenticity

1. Be Transparent

Honesty isn't just the best policy; it's the only policy. Be upfront about your products, services, and limitations. If something goes wrong, own it. Transparency shows that your brand values integrity over appearances, which fosters trust.

2. Stay True to Your Values

Authenticity means aligning your actions with your words. If you claim to support sustainability, ensure your practices reflect that. Customers are quick to spot inconsistencies, and staying true to your values shows that your brand walks the talk.

3. Show Your Human Side

People trust people, not faceless corporations. Share your brand's story, highlight the people behind the scenes, and communicate in a way that feels personal and genuine. Whether it's a handwritten thank-you note or a behind-the-scenes video, humanizing your brand goes a long way in building trust.

Creating a Lasting Impression

While trust earns loyalty, creating a memorable impression ensures that your brand is not just noticed but remembered. It's not enough to simply deliver good products or services—you need to be unforgettable. One way to achieve this is through consistency. When your branding—visuals, tone, and messaging—remains cohesive across all touchpoints, it fosters recognition and reliability. Customers come to expect the same high-quality experience every time they interact with your brand, reinforcing their confidence in you.

Another way to leave an impression is by delivering exceptional experiences. Every interaction, from the first click on your website to the moment a customer opens their package, should be designed to delight. Thoughtful details, like elegant packaging, a personalized note, or a quick and friendly follow-up email, can elevate a standard experience into something extraordinary.

Emotion also plays a crucial role in making your brand memorable. People are far more likely to remember how you made them feel than what you sold them. Whether it's through a heartfelt customer service exchange, an ad campaign that tugs at the heartstrings, or a humorous social media post, creating emotional moments leaves a lasting impact.

Finally, telling your brand's story can give it depth and relatability. Stories are sticky—they linger in people's minds and help them connect with your brand on a personal level. Sharing your journey, mission, or the tangible ways your product impacts lives adds richness and makes your brand stand out from the crowd.

By focusing on consistency, exceptional experiences, emotional resonance, and compelling storytelling, your brand can create impressions that last long after the first interaction, ensuring you're remembered for all the right reasons.

The Trust-Impression Cycle: The Dynamic Duo of Brand Success

Trust and a lasting impression are like peanut butter and jelly—they're amazing on their own but absolutely magical together. They don't just coexist; they work hand in hand to turn casual customers into loyal superfans. Trust is what makes people feel safe choosing your brand, while memorable impressions are what keep you lodged in their minds (and hearts). Together, they create an unstoppable cycle of loyalty and advocacy that drives your brand's growth and keeps customers coming back for more.

Let's break it down. Imagine a customer's first interaction with your brand. Maybe they stumble upon your website or see an ad on social media. Your visuals, messaging, and tone create that initial impression. If it's fresh, engaging, and memorable, they'll be intrigued enough to stick around. But that's just the beginning—this is where trust steps in. If your website is easy to navigate, your reviews are glowing, and your promises feel credible, you're already building trust before they even make a purchase.

Fast-forward to the actual transaction: they've placed their order, and now it's time for you to deliver. If their package arrives on time, beautifully packaged, and maybe even with a little surprise tucked inside, you're not just meeting their expectations—you're exceeding them. This leaves a powerful impression that goes beyond the product itself. And when you pair that with consistent quality and genuine communication, trust takes root.

But here's the fun part: trust and impression feed off each other. When customers trust your brand, they're more open to engaging with your content, trying new products, and recommending you to others. Each positive interaction reinforces their trust and deepens the impression you've left. On the flip side, when your brand consistently goes above and beyond, it leaves an indelible mark that strengthens their trust even further. It's a cycle that keeps spinning, creating loyal customers who rave about your brand to anyone who'll listen.

And let's not forget the cherry on top—advocacy. When customers feel both trust and delight, they don't just remain buyers; they become your biggest cheerleaders. They'll share glowing reviews, post about you on social media, and bring their friends along for the ride. In this way, the trust-impression cycle doesn't just sustain your brand; it propels it forward.

So, think of trust as the foundation and lasting impressions as the sparkle. Together, they create a brand experience that's as solid as it is memorable. Build trust with authenticity and consistency, deliver unforgettable moments at every turn, and watch as the cycle spins your brand into a league of its own. Because when you master the trust-impression duo, you're not just playing the game—you're winning it.

Building trust and leaving a lasting impression is the cornerstone of a successful brand. It's about showing up consistently, delivering exceptional experiences, and being authentic in everything you do. When customers trust your brand and carry a positive impression of it, they're not just buying products—they're investing in a relationship. And in today's fast-moving world, that's the kind of connection that turns a business into a beloved brand.

?

CHAPTER NINE

PERSONALIZATION AT SCALE

Using Data and Insights to Craft Tailored Customer Experiences

In a world where customers are bombarded with generic ads, cookie-cutter emails, and one-size-fits-all solutions, personalization is the game-changer that makes your brand stand out. It's no longer enough to treat customers as part of a crowd—they want to feel seen, understood, and valued. Enter personalization at scale, the art and science of using data and insights to create tailored experiences for every customer, without losing efficiency. It's how you make a big brand feel personal, creating connections that drive loyalty and trust.

Why Personalization Matters?

Imagine walking into a store, and instead of a generic greeting, the staff knows your name, remembers your favorite products, and suggests something they know you'll love. You'd feel pretty special, right? That's the magic of personalization. It turns everyday interactions into memorable moments. Customers aren't just looking for products—they're looking for brands that get them. When you personalize their experience, you show that your brand understands their preferences, anticipates their needs, and genuinely cares.

But here's the kicker: today's consumers expect this kind of treatment everywhere. Whether they're shopping online, browsing an app, or opening an email, they want brands to know them—without being creepy about it. Personalization bridges the gap between customer expectations and brand offerings, delivering experiences that feel seamless and human.

The Role of Data in Personalization

Personalization at scale starts with data—the fuel that powers tailored customer experiences. Every click, purchase, review, and interaction generates valuable insights. By analyzing this data, brands can uncover customer preferences, behaviors, and pain points. For example:

Purchase history shows what they like and how often they buy.

Browsing behavior reveals what products catch their eye.

Location data helps tailor offerings based on regional trends or seasons.

Feedback and reviews highlight what's working and what's not.

But raw data alone isn't enough. It needs to be transformed into actionable insights. Advanced tools like AI and machine learning can process massive amounts of data, identifying patterns and predicting future behaviors. These insights enable brands to craft hyper-relevant experiences for each customer while maintaining efficiency.

Crafting Tailored Experiences at Scale

Dynamic Content

Personalization shines brightest when content feels like it was made for the individual. Emails that address customers by name, recommend products based on past purchases, or highlight deals in their region create a sense of connection. Even websites can adapt dynamically, showcasing products or content based on user behavior.

Customized Offers and Discounts

Blanket sales are a thing of the past. Personalized discounts based on shopping history or loyalty can make customers feel valued. For example, offering a discount on a product they've been eyeing or rewarding frequent buyers with exclusive perks strengthens the relationship.

Behavior-Based Recommendations

Think about the "You might also like" suggestions on streaming platforms or online stores. These recommendations, powered by data, make customers feel like the brand understands their preferences, leading to increased engagement and sales.

Seamless Omni-Channel Experiences

Personalization isn't limited to one platform. When a customer starts browsing on your website, adds items to their cart, and then switches to your app, the experience should feel connected. Reminders, saved preferences, and consistent messaging ensure a smooth journey across channels.

Interactive Tools

Quizzes, chatbots, and virtual assistants powered by customer data can provide tailored advice, from recommending skincare products to helping them choose the perfect vacation package. These tools add value by making decision-making easier and more enjoyable.

The Challenges of Personalization at Scale

While personalization sounds like the perfect strategy, scaling it comes with challenges. Managing massive amounts of data securely and ethically is a top priority. Customers expect personalization, but they also value their privacy. Striking the right balance between helpful and intrusive is key. Transparency about how you use data and giving customers control over their preferences builds trust.

Additionally, scaling personalization requires robust technology. Investing in tools like AI, CRM platforms, and marketing automation is essential to handle the complexity of tailoring experiences for large audiences. Finally, consistency is critical—personalization efforts should feel seamless across every touchpoint, from email campaigns to in-store interactions.

Personalization at scale is no longer a "nice-to-have"—it's a must-have in today's customer-centric world. By leveraging data and insights, brands can create tailored experiences that feel personal, even when reaching millions of customers. It's about making every interaction meaningful, relevant, and human. When you get it right, you're not just meeting expectations—you're exceeding them. And that's how you turn customers into loyal advocates who keep coming back for more. So, start personalizing, start connecting, and watch your brand's impact scale to new heights.

Brands that excel at personalization

- *Spotify – Personalized Playlists for Every User*

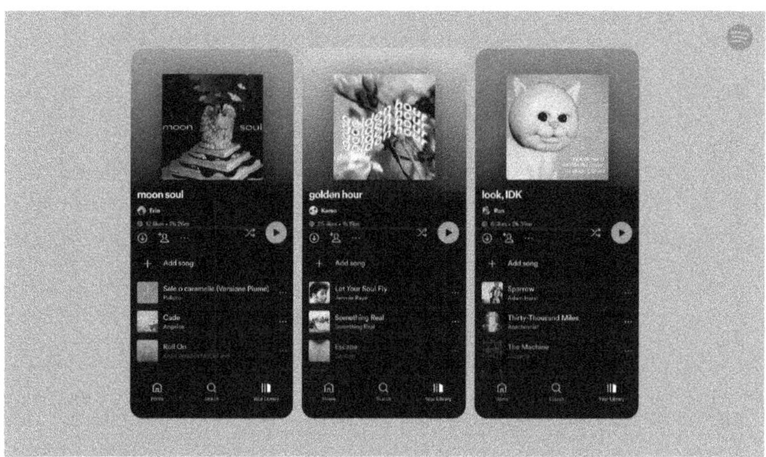

Spotify now lets you create and customise your own playlist covers, in-app

Overview: Spotify has revolutionized the way people consume music by offering personalized experiences that make users feel like each playlist, recommendation, and interaction is designed just for them. By leveraging vast amounts of user data and sophisticated machine learning algorithms, Spotify has become a leader in personalized content in the streaming industry. Its ability to curate music suggestions and playlists based on individual preferences is one of the key reasons for its massive growth and user retention.

Implementation:

Spotify's personalized experience is driven by its ability to track and analyze users' listening habits, behaviors, and even contextual factors like time of day or location. The company uses a combination of collaborative filtering, natural language processing, and audio analysis to power its personalized features.

Discover Weekly: One of the most popular personalized features on Spotify is Discover Weekly. This feature creates a personalized playlist for each user every Monday, based on their listening history, as well as patterns observed in other users with similar tastes. By analyzing the songs a user listens to, the system can recommend music that fits their taste, while still introducing them to new artists or genres that they might enjoy.

How It Works: The algorithm tracks your listening habits, identifying songs and genres you often play. It then finds patterns in other users who share similar music preferences and uses these to recommend songs you haven't heard before but are likely to enjoy.

Impact: Since its launch, Discover Weekly has become a staple for Spotify users, resulting in increased engagement and time spent on the platform. According to Spotify, around 40% of Spotify users listen to the Discover Weekly playlist each week, leading to higher user retention and satisfaction.

Daily Mixes: Spotify also offers personalized playlists in the form of Daily Mixes. These mixes are generated every day and are based on the user's listening behavior, mixing familiar tracks with some new songs they may like. The algorithm analyzes the type of music the user listens to most frequently and adjusts the playlist accordingly, providing a perfect balance of favorite tracks and fresh recommendations.

How It Works: Each day, Spotify delivers a new mix with songs the user has already played frequently, along with recommendations of similar tracks. Multiple Daily Mixes are created based on the user's various listening habits, offering tailored music for different moods or activities.

Impact: This feature keeps users engaged by regularly offering fresh music that aligns with their tastes, leading to a higher frequency of app usage. The dynamic, daily nature of the playlist also keeps users coming back to the app to discover new content.

Spotify Wrapped: Another hugely successful feature is Spotify Wrapped, an annual recap that highlights users' top songs, genres, and artists of the year. Spotify Wrapped is based on user data collected throughout the year, offering personalized insights into listening habits and preferences. Wrapped is not only a fun and personalized feature, but it also serves as a tool to drive user engagement and social sharing.

How It Works: Spotify gathers detailed data on users' listening patterns over the course of the year, including top tracks, artists, and genres. At the end of the year, it curates a visual, shareable summary for users, allowing them to reflect on their music journey.

Impact: Spotify Wrapped is widely shared on social media platforms, creating viral buzz and driving new user sign-ups. Wrapped has become a cultural moment each December, with users eagerly awaiting the personalized stats. This feature creates a deeper emotional connection with users and encourages social sharing, which increases brand visibility and draws in new customers.

Contextual Personalization: Spotify goes beyond just analyzing listening history by integrating contextual data into its personalization strategy. For instance, Spotify analyzes factors such as the time of day, location, and even the device being used to deliver contextually relevant music. This is especially seen in features like Spotify Runningand Spotify's Mood Playlists, where the platform adapts music recommendations to the user's physical activity or emotional state.

How It Works: When a user selects "Spotify Running," the app matches the tempo of the music to the pace of the user's running speed. Similarly, when users select mood-based playlists (e.g., "Happy," "Chill," or "Focus"), Spotify curates tracks that match the user's emotional state based on historical listening patterns.

Impact: This contextual approach creates a seamless user experience, where the music feels aligned not only with the user's personal preferences but also with their real-time needs.

Results:

Spotify's personalization strategy has been one of the key drivers behind its success and expansion. Personalized playlists, such as Discover Weekly and Daily Mix, contribute significantly to the platform's user engagement and retention. As of 2021, Spotify had more than 365 million active users and 165 million paid subscribers (Spotify, 2021), a direct result of its ability to create customized experiences that keep users engaged.

The success of Discover Weekly alone, with 40% of users listening to it each week, showcases the effectiveness of personalized playlists in increasing user satisfaction. Additionally, Spotify Wrapped has not only become a social media phenomenon but has also helped the platform stay top of mind for users year after year.

Challenges and Areas for Improvement:

While Spotify's personalized features have been a massive success, the company faces the challenge of continually improving its algorithms to stay relevant and avoid predictability. As personalization becomes a common feature in the music streaming industry, the need for continual innovation grows. Additionally, some users may feel overwhelmed by the sheer volume of recommendations or dislike the feeling of being "too catered to." Finding a balance between personalization and user control is crucial for maintaining long-term satisfaction.

Conclusion:

Spotify's success in personalizing the music experience has made it a leader in the entertainment industry. By analyzing user data and creating playlists that evolve with individual preferences, Spotify ensures its users are not just passive listeners but active participants in their music discovery journey. Its personalized approach not only keeps users engaged but also helps foster deeper connections with the brand. Spotify's use of data and insights has transformed the music industry by making each user's experience feel unique and special, which is why the platform continues to grow year after year.

"*Reference:*
Spotify. (2021). Spotify Annual Report 2021. Retrieved from https://www.spotify.com/us/about-us/"

Starbucks: Personalized Rewards That Brew Loyalty

Starbucks Loyalty Program

Starbucks has long been a leader in creating memorable customer experiences, and a significant part of its success lies in its use of personalized rewards through its Starbucks Rewards Program. By combining advanced data analytics, mobile technology, and a deep understanding of customer preferences, Starbucks has built a loyalty program that not only drives repeat visits but also strengthens emotional connections with its customers.

How Starbucks Leverages Personalization?

Mobile App Integration

The Starbucks Rewards Program is seamlessly integrated into the Starbucks mobile app, making it convenient for customers to engage with the program. Customers can order ahead, pay using the app, and collect stars (the program's reward points) with every purchase. The app also tracks their order history, enabling

Starbucks to make personalized recommendations based on past purchases.

Tailored Promotions and Offers

Starbucks uses customer data to send targeted promotions, such as discounts on frequently purchased items or incentives to try new seasonal beverages. For example, if a customer regularly orders a latte, they might receive an offer for a discounted latte on their next visit or a bonus stars promotion when they buy a new variant of their favorite drink.

Behavior-Driven Engagement

Starbucks ensures that its messaging feels personal by analyzing customer behavior. For instance, if a customer hasn't visited in a while, the app might send a "We miss you" notification with a special offer to encourage them to return. Similarly, during a customer's birthday month, the app delivers a free drink offer, adding a celebratory and thoughtful touch.

Customized Menus

The app's menu adapts to the user, prioritizing items they are likely to purchase. If someone frequently orders non-dairy milk, the app might highlight almond milk-based drinks or suggest adding oat milk to new beverages.

Gamification

Starbucks incorporates gamified elements into its rewards program to make it more engaging. Bonus stars challenges, double-star days, and seasonal rewards campaigns create excitement and incentivize frequent participation. Customers are motivated to spend more to reach higher star thresholds and unlock rewards.

The Impact of Personalized Rewards

Customer Loyalty

The personalization offered by the Starbucks Rewards Program fosters a deep sense of loyalty. Customers feel recognized and valued when the brand remembers their preferences and tailors offers specifically for them. According to Schultz (2019), Starbucks Rewards members account for nearly 50% of the company's sales in the U.S., highlighting the program's effectiveness in driving loyalty.

Increased Engagement

Personalized rewards keep customers engaged with the brand. The convenience of the mobile app, coupled with timely offers and gamified elements, ensures that customers remain actively involved. Starbucks reported a significant increase in mobile app adoption and in-app orders, driven by the rewards program (Starbucks Corporation, 2020).

Higher Average Spend

Starbucks Rewards members tend to spend more per transaction compared to non-members. The incentive to earn stars, combined with personalized offers, encourages members to purchase additional items or upgrade their orders. A report by Forbes highlighted that personalized promotions resulted in a 20% increase in average order value among Rewards members (Gartenberg, 2019).

Enhanced Brand Loyalty

By consistently delivering personalized experiences, Starbucks strengthens its emotional connection with customers. Customers view the brand not just as a coffee chain but as a part of their daily routines and celebrations.

Lessons from Starbucks' Personalization Strategy

- Embrace Technology: Invest in a robust app that makes participation seamless and enjoyable.

- Leverage Data Responsibly: Use customer data to enhance experiences but ensure transparency and security.

- Create Emotional Touchpoints: Add personal touches, such as birthday rewards or "We miss you" messages, to build emotional connections.

- Incorporate Gamification: Make loyalty programs engaging and fun to encourage repeat interactions.

- Be Consistent Across Channels: Ensure that personalization extends across in-store, online, and mobile experiences.

Conclusion

Starbucks' Rewards Program is a masterclass in how to use personalization to drive loyalty and customer engagement. By integrating advanced technology, tailoring offers, and creating emotional connections, Starbucks has turned its rewards program into a key driver of its success. It serves as a blueprint for other brands aiming to create meaningful and lasting relationships with their customers through personalization.

"*References*

Gartenberg, C. (2019). How Starbucks uses data to increase customer loyalty. Forbes. Retrieved from https://www.forbes.com

Schultz, H. (2019). From the Ground Up: A Journey to Reimagine the Promise of Starbucks. New York, NY: Random House.

Starbucks Corporation. (2020). Annual Report: Driving Customer Engagement through Technology and Personalization. Retrieved from https://www.starbucks.com"

Mastering the Art of Disruption

CHAPTER TEN

Challenging Industry Norms

Challenging Industry Norms: Lessons from Brands That Broke All the Rules (and Won)

Let's get one thing straight: playing it safe is so last century. The brands that make waves today aren't following the rules—they're rewriting them. Disruptive brands don't tiptoe into an industry; they kick the door open, shake things up, and leave everyone wondering, "Why didn't we think of that?" They don't just improve the status quo—they obliterate it and create something entirely new. Let's dive into what makes these rule-breaking brands so legendary and what you can learn from their playbook.

What Does It Mean to Challenge Industry Norms?

Challenging industry norms is like looking at a line of people doing the same boring thing and saying, "Yeah, no thanks." It's about spotting inefficiencies, outdated practices, or downright frustrating customer experiences and flipping them on their heads. Disruptive brands don't just tweak the old—they invent the new.

Take Airbnb, for example. While traditional hotels were busy offering mini shampoos and overpriced room service, Airbnb asked, "What if travelers want something more personal?" By connecting people to homes instead of hotel rooms, they didn't just disrupt the travel industry—they redefined it.

Lessons from Brands That Said "Let's Do It Differently"

1. Solve Real Problems (And Don't Overcomplicate)

Disruptive brands don't aim to dazzle with fluff—they fix what's broken and simplify life for their customers.

- **What You Can Learn:** Look for pain points specific to your audience and solve them in ways no one else is.

- **Example:** Paytm revolutionized payments in India by addressing the need for secure, cashless transactions. With its user-friendly interface and quick adoption of UPI, Paytm made digital payments accessible to millions, including small businesses and rural users.

2. Redefine the Rules

Indian disruptors succeed by not playing the same old game. They rewrite the rulebook to fit modern needs.

- **What You Can Learn:** Challenge outdated practices and offer something refreshing and relevant.

- **Example:** Ola took the Indian cab industry for a spin—literally. Instead of relying on outdated booking systems and unreliable services, they created a tech-savvy platform that made booking rides as easy as tapping your screen. With innovations like Ola Auto and Ola Electric, they've continued to evolve, setting new benchmarks in mobility.

3. Let Technology Do the Heavy Lifting

Technology isn't just for nerds in lab coats; it's the secret sauce for disrupting industries. The smartest brands use tech to make their customers' lives easier, faster, or just plain cooler.

- **What You Can Learn:** Embrace technology to streamline processes and wow your customers.

- **Example:** Netflix didn't just see the future of entertainment—they streamed it. By swapping DVDs for instant access to movies and shows, they turned binge-watching into a lifestyle. Bonus points for using algorithms to recommend your next favorite show before you even know you want it.

4. Build Communities, Not Just Customers

Disruptive brands don't just sell—they create movements that make their customers feel part of something bigger.

- **What You Can Learn:** Align your brand with values and causes that resonate with your audience to foster loyalty.

- **Example:** Bombay Shaving Company built a community around self-care and premium grooming. With campaigns that celebrated individuality and thoughtful packaging that felt like a gift, they didn't just sell razors—they built a lifestyle brand.

5. Be Bold, Even When It's Risky

Taking risks is in every disruptor's DNA. You can't shake up an industry without ruffling a few feathers.

- **What You Can Learn:** Dare to take bold steps, but ensure they're backed by research and customer insight.

- **Example:** Zomato started as a restaurant discovery platform and took a leap into food delivery, challenging established players. With quirky, relatable marketing and innovations like Zomato Gold, they didn't just compete—they became synonymous with food delivery in India.

6. Make Customer Experience King

Disruptive brands understand that great products aren't enough—they need to deliver exceptional experiences that customers rave about.

- **What You Can Learn:** Focus on creating seamless, delightful experiences at every touchpoint.

- **Example:** Nykaa revolutionized beauty retail by offering a curated shopping experience, both online and offline. Their detailed product descriptions, personalized recommendations, and emphasis on inclusivity created a brand that feels like a trusted friend guiding you through your beauty journey.

Why Disruption Isn't Always Easy?

Disrupting an industry in India comes with unique challenges—regulatory hurdles, diverse customer preferences, and stiff competition from established players. For instance, companies like Swiggy had to tackle logistical challenges in India's crowded cities and unpredictable traffic conditions. The lesson? Disruption isn't about a smooth ride; it's about persistence and adaptability.

Be the Brand That Asks, "Why Not?"

Brands like Flipkart, Paytm, Netflix, and Nykaa didn't just challenge industry norms—they shattered them. They saw inefficiencies, understood local needs, and dared to do things differently. Whether it was digitizing payments, redefining education, or transforming personal care, these brands showed that disruption starts with asking bold questions and ends with making customers' lives better.

So, take a page from these innovators' playbooks. Identify what's broken, reimagine what could be, and don't be afraid to shake things up. Who knows—you might just be the next Indian brand to leave competitors in the dust and create something truly remarkable. ?

How to Take Risks and Stand Apart?

Why Take Risks?

Playing it safe keeps you in the pack, but taking risks puts you ahead. Bold moves help your brand break free from mediocrity, capture attention, and stay top of mind. Risks often come with rewards—disruption, differentiation, and the loyalty of customers who see you as an innovator. Without risk, there's no real growth, and you risk being overshadowed by competitors who dare to think differently.

How to Take Risks While Challenging Norms?

Taking risks doesn't mean flipping a coin and hoping for the best—it's about spotting real problems and tackling them in unconventional ways. Successful risk-takers identify the gaps or pain points in their industry and think creatively about how to address them. For instance, **Durex India** didn't just sell condoms—they shattered taboos around sexual health with bold, witty campaigns that resonated with younger audiences. Their risks weren't random; they were calculated moves that addressed societal barriers while making people laugh.

Of course, being bold doesn't mean being reckless. Smart brands do their homework before taking the plunge. Research your audience, test your ideas, and back your risks with solid insights. Bold moves should feel daring to the world but carefully calculated to you. Start small, perhaps with a pilot program or test campaign, and use the feedback to refine your approach. Think of it like dipping your toe in before cannonballing into the deep end—it's still fun, but way smarter.

Another key to standing out? Embrace your unique identity unapologetically. Your brand's quirks and differences are its superpower. **Paper Boat** nailed this by stepping away from the typical fizzy drink formula and offering nostalgic beverages like Aam Panna and Jaljeera. They didn't just sell drinks; they sold memories, complete with heartfelt storytelling that made every sip feel like a trip down memory lane.

Risk-takers also know how to create cultural moments. Instead of jumping on the latest trends, they start conversations that matter. Take **Tata Tea's iconic "Jaago Re"** campaign—it wasn't just about selling tea; it sparked dialogue about civic responsibility. By aligning your brand with bold ideas or movements, you don't just sell a product—you build cultural relevance that makes people sit up and take notice.

And here's the thing: not every risk will pay off, and that's okay. The most successful brands embrace failure as part of the process. Think of failure as feedback—each misstep teaches you what doesn't work and brings you closer to what does. Celebrate the lessons learned and don't shy away from sharing them. Customers love a brand that's transparent and human, one that says, "Hey, we tried this, it flopped, but here's what we learned." It makes you relatable and builds trust.

So, take those risks! Solve problems, embrace your identity, create moments that matter, and don't fear the occasional stumble. Because when you take bold steps while challenging norms, you're not just playing the game—you're rewriting it. ?

How to Stand Apart While Taking Risks?

Standing apart doesn't mean being so different that people don't get you—it's about being fresh while staying relatable. The magic lies in giving your audience something new and exciting without losing that connection to their needs. Think of **Amul's famous ads.** Their witty takes on current events are bold, sometimes risky, but always hit home because they tap into what people are already talking about. The brand's creativity and relevance make it impossible to ignore, proving you can challenge norms while staying relatable.

Next, it's not just about creating groundbreaking products—it's about rethinking how customers experience them. **Swiggy** didn't invent food delivery, but they turned it into an art. From real-time tracking to genius campaigns like **#WhatTheFalooda**, they transformed a simple service into a delightful experience. So, ask yourself: how can you take what everyone's doing and make it feel like a joyride for your customers?

Authenticity is your secret weapon when it comes to taking risks. It's tempting to jump on every shiny new trend, but staying true to your brand's core is what keeps you unique. Take **Khadi India**, for example. Instead of chasing modern design trends, they doubled down on their roots—**traditional fabrics and artisanal craftsmanship**—and turned those into a global statement of sustainability and heritage. The lesson? Be bold, but make sure your boldness feels you.

Don't shy away from risky marketing. Sometimes, a bold message is exactly what your audience needs to hear. Take Tanishq's campaign celebrating interfaith harmony—it sparked conversations, challenged societal norms, and beautifully tied into their brand ethos of celebrating love in all its forms. Sure, it came with its share of controversy, but the risks they took resonated deeply with their audience, proving that powerful storytelling can go a long way.

> "*Balancing Risk with Responsibility*
>
> *While taking risks is essential, it's equally important to ensure they align with ethical practices and customer trust. Missteps can damage your reputation, so it's vital to stay transparent, inclusive, and respectful in your bold moves. Risks should elevate your brand, not alienate your audience.*"

Taking risks and challenging norms isn't about being reckless—it's about being fearless in pursuing innovation and differentiation. The brands that stand apart are the ones that see opportunities where others see limits, address challenges head-on, and connect with their audiences in meaningful ways.

So, dare to be bold. Take the calculated leap. Stand apart by solving problems, embracing your identity, and turning risks into rewards. Because when you challenge the status quo, you don't just enter the game—you change it entirely.

CHAPTER ELEVEN

Leveraging Innovation for Uniqueness

Using Technology and Creativity to Stay Ahead

In today's fast-evolving world, staying ahead of the competition requires more than just good ideas—it demands innovation. Leveraging technology and creativity is how brands transform from ordinary to extraordinary. It's about going beyond what's expected, finding new ways to delight customers, and creating an identity that others can't replicate. When you blend cutting-edge tech with a creative mindset, you don't just stay in the game—you lead it.

Why Innovation is Essential for Uniqueness?

Innovation is what keeps your brand fresh, relevant, and memorable. It allows you to solve problems in ways that others haven't thought of, creating products, services, or experiences that feel truly unique. But innovation isn't just about inventing the next big thing; it's also about constantly improving, rethinking processes, and enhancing customer experiences to make them feel effortless, enjoyable, and irreplaceable.

How to Use Technology for Innovation?

Let's face it: repetitive tasks are creativity killers. That's where automation swoops in like a superhero, saving the day by handling the mundane stuff so your team can focus on the big ideas. Imagine Domino's Pizza with its "Domino's Tracker." They didn't just automate pizza delivery updates—they turned waiting into an interactive experience. Suddenly, watching your pizza journey from "prepping" to "on its way" became part of the fun. That's automation done right: efficient, creative, and engaging.

Then there's AI and machine learning—the tech equivalent of a crystal ball. These tools don't just predict the future; they create personalized experiences that make customers feel like VIPs. Netflix is the perfect example. Their algorithms analyze every click, pause, and binge session to serve up shows you didn't even know you wanted to watch. It's like having your own personal movie concierge. Who wouldn't want that?

And let's not forget the magic of AR and VR, where the lines between the virtual and real world blur into something extraordinary. Lenskart nailed this with their AR try-on feature, letting you see how glasses look on your face without ever leaving your couch. It's innovative, convenient, and feels just a little bit like you're living in the future.

So, whether you're automating the boring bits, using AI to read minds (in a non-creepy way), or giving customers a virtual playground to explore your products, technology is your ultimate sidekick in the quest for innovation. ?

How Creativity Drives Innovation?

Creativity isn't always about inventing something brand new—it's often about finding fresh ways to present what you already have. Take storytelling, for example. It's not just about the tale you tell but how you tell it. Think of Fevicol's quirky ads that turn a humble glue into the hero of hilarious, relatable stories. From elephants stuck to buses to unbreakable bonds, their creative storytelling keeps them unforgettable without ever changing the product itself.

Then there's the magic of rethinking how customers experience your brand. It's not just about the end product—it's about every step they take to get there. Remember Swiggy Genie? They turned mundane tasks like delivering forgotten keys or picking up groceries into a lifesaver service, with witty branding that made even errands feel fun. By reimagining the customer journey, they didn't just meet expectations—they exceeded them with a creative twist.

And let's not forget bold product design, where form meets function in the most eye-catching way. Think of Titan Raga watches—elegant, striking, and unmistakably unique. Their intricate designs aren't just timepieces; they're wearable works of art that make you want to show them off. It's proof that a splash of creativity in design can transform products into icons.

So, whether it's crafting a story that sticks, reinventing how customers interact with your brand, or making designs that wow, creativity is the spark that turns good ideas into unforgettable ones.

Balancing Technology with Human Creativity

Innovation thrives at the intersection of technology and creativity. Technology provides the tools, but it's human creativity that gives those tools purpose and meaning. The key is to balance the efficiency of tech with the emotional connection that creativity brings. A chatbot might solve customer issues faster, but it's the witty or empathetic tone it uses that makes the interaction memorable.

Challenges of Leveraging Innovation

Of course, innovation comes with challenges. Technology can be expensive, and not every investment pays off. Creativity takes time and resources, and sometimes even the best ideas fail to connect with the audience. The key is to take calculated risks, learn from failures, and stay flexible enough to adapt when things don't go as planned.

Why Innovation is Worth It

When you leverage innovation effectively, your brand becomes more than a product or service—it becomes an experience. You build customer loyalty by constantly surprising and delighting your audience, and you create a competitive edge that others find hard to match.

Innovation is not a one-time act—it's a mindset. By combining the power of technology with boundless creativity, you can stay ahead of the curve, differentiate your brand, and deliver experiences that keep your customers coming back for more. So, embrace the tools of the future, add a dash of imagination, and let innovation take your brand to places it's never been before. ?

***Building exclusivity through personalization** is like throwing a VIP party where every guest feels like the star of the show. Imagine walking into a store, and instead of a generic greeting, you're welcomed by name, offered your favorite coffee, and shown products that seem like they were handpicked just for you—it's that magical feeling of being truly seen and valued. Brands that master personalization know that exclusivity isn't about keeping people out; it's about making the ones who are in feel extra special.*

Think of it as creating a club where every member gets the royal treatment. Personalization goes beyond slapping a customer's name on an email; it's about crafting experiences so tailored that customers feel they're the only ones that matter. Spotify gets this—they don't just recommend music; they curate playlists that make you think they've been eavesdropping on your most private karaoke sessions. Similarly, Nykaa makes shopping a breeze with recommendations based on past purchases, making every visit feel like a personal beauty consultation. But personalization doesn't just make people happy—it builds loyalty, because when a brand shows it "gets" you, why would you shop anywhere else? Even high-end brands like Louis Vuitton and Tesla use personalization to maintain their aura of exclusivity; a custom handbag or a tailored car experience isn't just a product—it's a statement that says, "This was made for me."

Technology is the secret sauce here, enabling brands to use data to anticipate needs and preferences. AI, machine learning, and predictive analytics make it possible to know your customer better than they know themselves. Amazon, for instance, doesn't just suggest what you might like—they make it hard to resist by showing you what you didn't even know you wanted. But building exclusivity isn't just about data—it's about emotion.

People love feeling unique, and when brands personalize with empathy—whether it's by acknowledging their birthday, rewarding loyalty, or sending a heartfelt thank-you note—it turns a transaction into a relationship. Of course, there's a balance to strike. Go overboard, and you might creep people out; stay too generic, and you risk being forgettable.

The trick is to create a sense of belonging while making the experience feel one-of-a-kind. It's about saying, "We know you" without crossing into "We know too much about you." Starbucks nails this with its app, remembering your favorite drink and offering personalized rewards, making every visit feel like a treat. And who can forget Apple, the master of exclusivity? Their stores, their packaging, even their product launches feel like you're joining a secret society of tech-savvy trendsetters.

Exclusivity through personalization is about building a sense of intimacy at scale, where every customer feels like they're getting the VIP treatment, even if millions of others are too. It's not just good business—it's pure magic. Whether you're customizing a product, tailoring an experience, or simply making someone's day brighter with a thoughtful touch, personalization is how you show your customers that they're not just another number—they're the number one.

CHAPTER TWELVE

SUSTAINABILITY AND SOCIAL IMPACT

How Modern Consumers Reward Purpose-Driven Brands

In today's world, consumers aren't just buying products—they're buying into values, missions, and the greater good. Modern shoppers care deeply about the impact their purchases have on the environment, society, and future generations. They're quick to reward purpose-driven brands that prioritize sustainability and social responsibility, often choosing them over competitors, even if it costs a little more. For these consumers, it's not just about what a brand sells—it's about what it stands for.

Why Purpose Matters to Consumers?

Consumers today are more informed and conscious than ever. They know the toll fast fashion takes on the environment, the human cost of exploitative labor, and the devastating effects of unsustainable practices on our planet. This heightened awareness has led to a demand for transparency, ethical practices, and brands that contribute positively to society. For many, buying from a purpose-driven brand is a way to align their spending with their personal values—whether it's reducing carbon footprints, supporting fair trade, or championing social causes.

When a brand takes a stand on issues that matter, it creates an emotional connection with its audience. People feel good knowing their money supports something bigger than themselves. Brands that take purpose seriously aren't just selling products; they're creating movements, building trust, and fostering loyalty.

Examples of Purpose-Driven Brands

- **Tata Group:** From sustainability-focused businesses like Tata Power to philanthropy initiatives through the Tata Trusts, this Indian conglomerate has shown that profits and purpose can go hand in hand.

- **The Body Shop:** This beauty brand has long championed cruelty-free products, ethical sourcing, and community trade, proving that business can be a force for good.

- **Levi's:** Known for its denim, Levi's is also recognized for its commitment to sustainability with water-saving practices, recycling initiatives, and programs to reduce waste.

How Consumers Reward Purpose-Driven Brands

When a brand genuinely cares about making a difference, consumers don't just buy from them—they stand by them. It's the kind of loyalty that runs deep, where customers don't just love the product; they love the purpose behind it. Take Patagonia, for example. Their environmental activism has turned customers into lifelong fans who not only wear their gear but proudly tell others, "This jacket helps save the planet!" That emotional connection creates advocates who return time and time again, not because they need a jacket but because they believe in the mission.

And let's talk about price. Purpose-driven brands often charge a bit more, but customers are more than happy to pay the extra bucks if it means supporting ethical practices and sustainable materials. Buying feels less like a transaction and more like a contribution to a better world. It's why people shell out for organic food, fair-trade coffee, or upcycled furniture—they're not just buying a product; they're investing in their values.

Then there's the word-of-mouth magic. People love sharing stories about brands doing good. Whether it's a company planting trees for every purchase or creating jobs for marginalized communities, these feel-good stories spread like wildfire. It's the kind of marketing money can't buy—free buzz fueled by consumers who can't stop raving about the positive impact.

And let's not forget trust. Transparency is the holy grail of purpose-driven brands. When companies openly share their efforts—whether it's reducing plastic waste or improving worker conditions—it builds credibility. Customers are savvy enough to spot a fake, so brands that "walk the talk" win big. It's the difference between a company saying, "We're eco-friendly" and one that backs it up with stats like, "We reduced our carbon footprint by 50% last year." Transparency doesn't just earn trust; it solidifies a lasting relationship.

> "*Purpose-driven brands aren't just selling products—they're creating movements, and consumers are more than ready to join in. It's a win-win: the planet gets a boost, society benefits, and customers feel like heroes*"

How to Build a Purpose-Driven Brand

1. Define Your Mission

Identify what your brand stands for and align it with issues your audience cares about. Your mission should be authentic, clear, and actionable.

2. Walk the Talk

Back up your promises with real action. Whether it's using sustainable materials, reducing waste, or supporting local communities, your efforts need to reflect your mission.

3. Be Transparent

Share your journey, including your successes and challenges. Transparency builds trust and shows that your brand is genuinely committed to making a difference.

4. Engage Your Audience

Involve your customers in your mission. Encourage them to participate in campaigns, share their stories, or contribute to causes you support.

5. Measure and Share Impact

Highlight the tangible results of your efforts—whether it's trees planted, waste reduced, or lives impacted. This reinforces your credibility and motivates your audience to continue supporting you.

Sustainability and social impact are no longer optional—they're essential for building trust, loyalty, and long-term success. Modern consumers want to support brands that reflect their values and contribute to a better world. By prioritizing purpose over profit, businesses can create meaningful connections with their audience while driving positive change. It's not just good for the planet—it's good for business. After all, when you stand for something that matters, you don't just sell products—you inspire movements. ?

Making an Impact While Staying Profitable

Running a business isn't just about the bottom line anymore. Today, companies are expected to do more than rake in profits; they're expected to make a difference. But here's the catch: how do you create meaningful impact without draining your bank account? The good news is that making an impact and staying profitable aren't mutually exclusive—they're two sides of the same shiny coin. Think of it as the business world's version of having your cake and eating it too (preferably a sustainably sourced, fair-trade cake). The secret lies in weaving purpose into your profit strategy so seamlessly that they lift each other up, instead of fighting for attention.

Take brands like Toms Shoes, for example. They pioneered the "One for One" model, giving a pair of shoes to someone in need for every pair sold. On the surface, it seems altruistic, but dig deeper, and you'll see the brilliance: the feel-good factor drives sales. Customers don't just buy shoes—they buy into the mission, turning compassion into a competitive advantage. This kind of impact-driven business model proves that profit and purpose aren't opposites; they're dance partners. The more you step up your impact game, the more your customers are likely to open their wallets, not just because they need your product, but because they want to support your cause.

But let's not stop at shoes. Even massive corporations like Unilever are proving you can be a global powerhouse and a force for good. Through their "Sustainable Living" plan, they're tackling everything from reducing emissions to sourcing materials ethically, all while staying wildly profitable. How? By building sustainability into their operations in ways that reduce costs and attract like-minded consumers. It's the perfect example of turning responsibility into revenue. And let's not forget the loyalty boost—a customer who feels your brand aligns with their values is more likely to stick around, even when the competition whispers sweet discounts in their ears.

Now, you might think, This all sounds nice for billion-dollar brands, but what about smaller businesses? Great question! Impact doesn't have to come with a billion-dollar price tag. The trick is starting with what aligns naturally with your brand. If you're a local café, maybe you commit to sourcing coffee beans from ethical farms and reducing single-use plastics. If you're a tech startup, perhaps you offer free workshops for underprivileged youth, bridging the digital divide. These efforts don't just make you feel good—they also differentiate you in the market, attracting customers who care about more than price tags.

Of course, staying profitable while making an impact means getting creative about how you measure success. Profit is still king (we're not running charities here), but impact becomes a close second. Modern consumers want transparency, so share your progress openly—how much waste you've reduced, how many lives you've touched, or how much carbon you've offset. When customers see tangible results, they're not just impressed—they become advocates. And those advocates? They're your best (and free!) marketing tool, spreading the word about how your business is making the world a better place.

But let's not pretend it's all rainbows and sunshine. Balancing impact and profit has its challenges. Sustainable materials often cost more, and social initiatives can strain your budget. However, think of these as investments rather than expenses. Ethical practices may cost a bit upfront, but they build trust, loyalty, and long-term profitability. Plus, with growing government incentives and consumer demand for responsible businesses, impact-driven strategies are becoming less of a "nice-to-have" and more of a competitive necessity.

The key is to start where you are and scale your efforts as you grow. Don't try to solve all the world's problems overnight. Pick one cause, integrate it into your business model, and make it your brand's superpower. Then, as your revenue grows, expand your impact. It's like planting a tree—start small, nurture it, and eventually, it'll grow into a mighty oak that benefits everyone around it.

And here's the kicker: making an impact isn't just good for the planet or society—it's good for morale. Employees who see their work contributing to something meaningful are happier, more engaged, and more likely to stick around. And happy employees? They're productivity gold. It's a ripple effect—your team feels good, your customers feel good, and your business thrives.

In the end, making an impact while staying profitable is about finding your sweet spot—the intersection of what your business does well, what your customers care about, and what the world needs. It's about showing that capitalism doesn't have to be cold-hearted; it can have a conscience. So, go ahead: dream big, start small, and remember that every step you take toward creating positive change isn't just good for the world—it's great for business.

Growth Strategies for Long-Term Success

CHAPTER THIRTEEN

Consistency vs. Evolution

How to Stay True to Your Brand While Evolving Over Time

Imagine your brand as a classic rock band. Consistency is the signature sound your fans love, the one they can instantly recognize and hum along to. Evolution, on the other hand, is dropping a new album that feels fresh without alienating your audience. Balancing the two is like walking a tightrope—stay too consistent, and you risk becoming stale; evolve too quickly, and you might lose what made your brand special in the first place. The secret lies in honoring your core identity while embracing the changes needed to stay relevant in a fast-moving world.

Consistency is your foundation, the unchanging heartbeat of your brand. It's the reason why Coca-Cola feels the same whether you're sipping it in Mumbai or Manhattan. Your logo, tone, mission, and values are what make you recognizable, trustworthy, and, let's be honest, comfortable for your audience. Customers need to know what to expect from you; it's how they build trust and loyalty. But consistency doesn't mean rigidity—it's about maintaining your essence while leaving room to innovate.

That's where evolution comes in. **Evolution** is about adapting to new trends, technologies, and audience expectations without losing your identity. Think of Apple: it started as a computer company but has evolved into a lifestyle brand selling everything from sleek phones to futuristic watches. Yet, through all its transformations, Apple's commitment to innovation, simplicity, and premium quality has remained unchanged. Evolution is about staying ahead of the curve and ensuring your brand continues to matter in a constantly shifting landscape.

The trick is to know what to hold onto and what to let go of. Your core values and mission? Non-negotiable. Your packaging design from 1992? Probably time for an upgrade. Take Cadbury, for example. It has kept its comforting, chocolatey identity intact while updating its packaging and marketing to appeal to a younger audience. They didn't abandon their legacy—they modernized it.

Another key to balancing consistency and evolution is listening to your audience. Your customers will tell you what's working and what feels outdated—if you're willing to pay attention. Social media, reviews, and feedback are treasure troves of insights. Remember when Instagram changed its logo, and the internet had a collective meltdown? It's proof that even small changes can have a big impact, and it's a reminder to evolve with care and consideration.

Evolution doesn't always mean big, flashy changes; sometimes, it's about subtle tweaks. Starbucks didn't overhaul its entire identity when it modernized its logo—it simply removed the wordmark, making the siren icon the star. It was a bold yet thoughtful move that kept the brand's identity intact while giving it a sleek, contemporary edge.

One of the biggest challenges in balancing consistency and evolution is internal resistance. Change can be scary, especially for teams that fear alienating loyal customers. But the key is communication—ensure everyone understands why change is necessary and how it aligns with the brand's long-term vision. It's easier to embrace evolution when it feels like a natural extension of your identity rather than a complete departure.

Consistency and evolution aren't opposing forces—they're partners in your brand's journey. Consistency ensures your audience knows who you are and what you stand for, while evolution ensures you stay relevant and exciting. The goal is to evolve thoughtfully, keeping your brand's essence intact while embracing opportunities to grow. After all, even the most iconic brands weren't built by standing still. So, keep your foundation strong, let your creativity soar, and show the world that staying true to your brand doesn't mean staying stuck in the past.

Avoiding the Pitfalls of Rebranding

Rebranding can feel like a glow-up moment for your brand—a chance to freshen things up, modernize your image, and capture new audiences. But when done carelessly, it can also backfire spectacularly, leaving your loyal customers confused, alienated, or downright angry. The challenge lies in balancing consistency and evolution so that your brand feels fresh without losing its identity.

Why Rebranding Feels Risky?

Your brand is your promise to your customers—it's how they recognize, trust, and connect with you. A sudden or poorly executed rebrand can feel like a betrayal, leaving customers wondering, What happened to the brand I loved? A drastic overhaul that strays too far from your core identity risks alienating loyal fans, while a half-hearted attempt at evolution can feel unnecessary or, worse, irrelevant.

Common Rebranding Pitfalls

1. Losing Your Core Identity

When brands attempt a complete overhaul, they risk abandoning the elements that made them special in the first place. Customers shouldn't have to play detective to figure out if they're still dealing with the same brand.

Pitfall Example: Gap's 2010 rebranding fiasco. The company swapped its iconic blue box logo for a minimalist design, sparking outrage among fans who saw it as a betrayal of the brand's heritage. Gap backtracked within a week, proving that a rebrand without purpose can do more harm than good.

Solution: Anchor your rebrand in your brand's core values. Keep the elements that are synonymous with your identity—be it a logo, a tagline, or a particular color palette—and build from there.

2. Fixing What Isn't Broken

Rebranding for the sake of rebranding can confuse customers. If your brand is already strong and recognizable, a major change can feel unnecessary and even damaging.

Pitfall Example: Tropicana's 2009 packaging redesign. The brand ditched its iconic orange-with-a-straw design for a plain box with a generic feel. Sales plummeted by 20% within two months, forcing Tropicana to revert to its original design.

Solution: Rebrand only when you're addressing a real need, like outdated visuals, evolving customer demographics, or a shift in your mission. If it ain't broke, don't fix it—just tweak it.

3. Ignoring Your Audience

A rebrand that doesn't consider the preferences and emotions of your audience can feel tone-deaf. Your customers are the heart of your brand, and leaving them out of the equation can lead to backlash.

Pitfall Example: Airbnb's 2014 logo redesign introduced the "Bélo" symbol, which was met with mixed reactions, ranging from mockery to confusion. While the logo ultimately gained acceptance, the initial rollout lacked sufficient context to explain the change to loyal users.

Solution: Involve your audience in the process. Conduct surveys, gather feedback, and use storytelling to explain the why behind the rebrand. Show them how the new look still aligns with their expectations.

4. Overcomplicating the Design

A rebrand should simplify and modernize, not confuse. Overly complex designs or abstract messaging can leave customers scratching their heads.

Pitfall Example: Yahoo's 2019 rebrand introduced a new logo that didn't resonate with users, who felt it lacked the charm and personality of its predecessor.

Solution: Stick to simplicity. Your rebrand should make your message clearer, not more convoluted. If you're changing a logo or tagline, ensure it communicates your brand's personality and values instantly.

5. Ignoring Internal Buy-In

Your team is as much a part of your brand as your customers are. A rebrand that doesn't align with internal culture or has no buy-in from employees can fall flat.

Pitfall Example: A company that launches a rebrand externally without educating its team may face internal resistance, confusion, and misalignment.

Solution: Involve your team early in the process. Train them on the new messaging, explain the rationale behind the change, and ensure they're ready to champion the rebrand.

How to Nail a Rebrand While Balancing Consistency and Evolution

Rebranding is like getting a makeover—you want to look fresh and modern, but you still want people to recognize you when they see you. It's a balancing act that combines staying true to your roots with embracing change, and nailing it requires a thoughtful approach. You can't just slap on a new logo and call it a day; a successful rebrand starts with purpose and ends with a cohesive, exciting identity that resonates with your audience. Here's how to do it without making your customers (or your team) wonder, What were they thinking?

First things first: define your "why." Rebranding isn't something you should do just because it sounds fun or you're bored of your current look. A clear purpose is the foundation of any great rebrand. Are you trying to modernize for a younger audience? Fix a reputation issue? Show that your brand has evolved? Whatever the reason, it should be compelling enough to guide every decision you make. For example, if you're modernizing, you might want to keep some elements of your old brand while giving it a sleek, updated twist. But if you're addressing a major reputation issue, you may need a more radical overhaul. Think of it like redecorating a house: are you painting the walls a new color or knocking down walls to create an open concept? Knowing the answer makes everything else easier.

Once you've nailed down your **"why,"** it's time to figure out what's worth keeping. Even if your brand needs a major shake-up, there are likely elements your customers already love and recognize. These could be your logo's colors, your tagline, or even your tone of voice. Take Coca-Cola, for example: their logo has evolved over time, but the iconic red-and-white color scheme and script font have remained consistent. These familiar elements anchor the brand in its heritage while allowing for fresh updates. It's like giving yourself a trendy haircut but keeping the same warm smile—people still know it's you.

Now comes the part most brands fumble: communication. If you're going to rebrand, you need to bring your audience along for the ride. Don't just spring a new logo on them one day without explanation—tell them why you're doing it, how it aligns with your mission, and what they can expect moving forward. Sharing the story behind the rebrand creates transparency and builds trust. It also turns your rebrand into an event, something customers can feel excited and involved in. Use social media, email newsletters, or even behind-the-scenes videos to show off the process and give people a sneak peek of what's coming. A rebrand is a big deal, so treat it like one!

But before you unleash your shiny new branding on the world, take it for a **test drive**. Pilot your designs or messaging with focus groups, longtime customers, or even your own team. Their feedback is invaluable—it's better to discover that your new logo is a little too abstract in a test group than after a full rollout. This testing phase allows you to make tweaks and ensure your rebrand feels right for your audience. Plus, it makes the whole process feel more collaborative, which is a win-win.

Finally, when you're ready to **launch**, make sure your new branding is consistent across every channel. Nothing says "we didn't think this through" like a new logo on your website and the old one lingering on your packaging. Your audience should experience the same cohesive identity everywhere, whether they're scrolling through your Instagram feed, browsing your website, or picking up a product in-store. This consistency reinforces recognition and trust, making the rebrand feel seamless rather than jarring.

Rebranding can be intimidating, but when done thoughtfully, it's an opportunity to strengthen your connection with your audience while showing them how your brand is growing and evolving. By starting with a clear purpose, keeping the elements that work, involving your audience, testing your ideas, and ensuring consistency, you can nail your rebrand without losing what makes your brand special. So, go ahead—freshen up, stand out, and show the world your brand's next chapter!

CHAPTER FOURTEEN

The Role of Customer Engagement

Fostering Loyalty Through Authentic Connections

Customer engagement is like that friend who always knows how to make you feel special—whether it's remembering your birthday, asking about your day, or showing up with snacks just because you are hungry. Brands that master engagement create these kinds of authentic connections, turning customers into loyal advocates. It's not about shouting the loudest or having the fanciest campaigns—it's about building relationships that feel real, personal, and meaningful. When done right, customer engagement doesn't just drive sales; it creates a community of people who genuinely want to stick around.

At its core, customer engagement is about interaction. It's the back-and-forth between you and your audience that builds trust and keeps them coming back for more. **But here's the kicker:** it has to feel authentic. People can spot a phony interaction a mile away, and nothing kills loyalty faster than insincerity. Whether it's a simple thank-you email, a quick response on social media, or a personalized recommendation, the key is to make every touchpoint feel thoughtful and human. Engagement isn't just marketing—it's a conversation, a relationship, a two-way street.

Take social media, for example. It's one of the best tools for real-time engagement. A witty tweet, a heartfelt reply, or a fun interactive poll can make customers feel like they're part of your brand's story. Brands like Zomato and Amul have nailed this with their playful, relatable posts that feel like they're written by a friend, not a corporate machine. These moments of engagement may seem small, but they add up, creating a sense of belonging and familiarity that keeps customers invested.

But customer engagement isn't just about social media banter. It's also about listening—*really listening.* When customers leave reviews, ask questions, or provide feedback, they're handing you gold. Responding to these insights not only improves your offerings but also shows that you care about what they have to say. It's a simple yet powerful way to foster trust. For example, many brands use surveys or feedback forms to gather insights, but the real magic happens when they share how they're acting on that feedback. It's like saying, "We heard you, and we're doing something about it." That's how you turn customers into collaborators.

Personalization also plays a massive role in engagement. When a brand remembers your preferences, suggests products you actually like, or sends a thoughtful message on your birthday, it shows that you're more than just a transaction—you're a valued individual. Starbucks nails this with its rewards app, which not only tracks your favorite drinks but also offers personalized deals that make you feel like a VIP. These little gestures go a long way in building emotional connections, and as we all know, emotions drive loyalty.

Then there's the power of community. Engaged customers don't just want to interact with your brand—they want to connect with each other. Creating spaces for customers to share their experiences, whether through user-generated content, forums, or events, fosters a sense of belonging. Apple, for instance, has built a loyal following not just because of its products but because of the community it has cultivated around creativity, innovation, and shared experiences. A customer who feels part of a tribe is far more likely to stick around.

Of course, engagement isn't a one-size-fits-all strategy. Different audiences respond to different approaches, and the key is understanding what resonates with your unique customer base. For some, it's all about humor and playfulness; for others, it's about sincerity and depth. The trick is to stay consistent with your brand's voice while tailoring your engagement to meet your audience's expectations.

Customer engagement isn't just a *buzzword*—it's the glue that holds your customer relationships together. It's about creating moments of connection, listening with intent, and showing up in ways that feel meaningful. When customers feel genuinely valued, they reward you with their loyalty, their advocacy, and yes, their wallets. So, go ahead: start the conversation, nurture those connections, and watch as your engaged customers become your biggest fans.

Using Feedback to Refine Your Brand

Customer feedback is like the GPS for your brand—it tells you where you're going right, where you're making wrong turns, and how to get back on track. Engaging with your customers and actively seeking their feedback isn't just a courtesy; it's a goldmine of insights waiting to be tapped. Feedback is the bridge between what you think your brand is doing and what your customers actually experience. When used effectively, it not only improves your products and services but also strengthens customer relationships, fosters loyalty, and ensures your brand evolves in a direction that resonates.

Why Feedback Matters?

No one knows your brand better than the people who interact with it daily—*your customers*. Their feedback offers a fresh perspective, highlighting things you may have overlooked or misunderstood. It's like getting free advice from the people who care most about your success. Whether it's a rave review, a constructive critique, or even an outright complaint, every piece of feedback is a chance to grow. Ignoring it is like tossing a treasure map because you don't like the handwriting.

Customers feel valued when they know their opinions matter. A simple "*We heard you!*" can go a long way in building trust and loyalty. It shows that your brand isn't just a faceless corporation—it's a team of people who listen, care, and act. And when customers see their feedback reflected in your improvements, it turns them into advocates. They're no longer just buyers; they're collaborators in your brand's journey.

Turning Feedback Into Action

Listen Without Defensiveness

It's tempting to brush off negative feedback or assume customers "*just don't get it.*" But every critique, no matter how harsh, is an opportunity to learn. Approach feedback with an open mind and a willingness to improve.

Spot the Patterns

Not all feedback requires immediate action, but recurring themes are a clear signal. If multiple customers mention that your app is glitchy or your packaging is frustrating, it's time to address those issues. Patterns point you to the areas where improvement will have the most impact.

Prioritize What Matters

Let's be real—you can't act on every piece of feedback. Use data and common sense to prioritize changes that will deliver the most value to your customers and align with your brand's goals.

Close the Loop

When you act on feedback, let your customers know. Whether it's a social media post, an email, or a product update announcement, saying "We made this change because of you!" makes customers feel heard and appreciated.

Using Feedback to Strengthen Your Brand

Customer feedback is like that brutally honest friend who tells you when your outfit is off but also cheers you on when you're killing it. It's a goldmine for improving your brand, especially when it comes to your products and services. When customers point out what's not working—like a clunky app feature or a product that doesn't quite live up to the hype—it's your chance to level up. Maybe they suggest a tweak you hadn't considered or highlight an area that's ripe for innovation. Taking their advice not only keeps your brand relevant but also shows you're listening and adapting to their needs.

But feedback isn't just about the tangible stuff—it's about how you talk about your brand too. Ever launched a tagline you thought was genius, only to find out your audience is scratching their heads? Yup, been there. Sometimes feedback reveals that your messaging isn't landing the way you hoped. Maybe it's too vague, too clever for its own good, or just plain confusing. Instead of doubling down, use that insight to refine and sharpen your communication so your audience knows exactly who you are and why they should love you.

Transparency is another feedback superpower. When you not only listen to what customers are saying but also show them how you're acting on it, you build trust. Share the behind-the-scenes stories about what you're improving, be upfront about challenges, and celebrate the wins based on their input. Customers love feeling like they're part of the process—it turns a transactional relationship into a partnership.

And let's not forget the critics. Negative feedback might sting, but it's an opportunity in disguise. Responding thoughtfully to complaints—whether it's a bad review or a snarky tweet—can turn a frustrated customer into a loyal advocate. People appreciate it when you own up to mistakes and make it clear you're working to fix them. It's like saying, "We hear you, and we care." Suddenly, a potential PR disaster becomes a chance to show your brand's humanity and earn some serious loyalty points.

> "*Challenges of Feedback-Driven Engagement*
>
> *Of course, feedback isn't always easy to manage. It can feel overwhelming, especially when there's a flood of opinions pointing in different directions. It's also tough to sift through emotional rants or vague comments to find actionable insights. The key is having a system in place to collect, analyze, and prioritize feedback while staying true to your brand's vision.*"

Customer feedback isn't just a tool—it's a compass. It guides your brand's evolution, ensuring you stay relevant, connected, and customer-centric. By engaging with feedback openly and actively, you turn your customers into co-creators of your brand's journey. The result? A stronger, smarter, and more beloved brand that doesn't just meet expectations—it exceeds them. So, listen, learn, and let feedback be the fuel that powers your brand forward.

CHAPTER FIFTEEN

Marketing Beyond the Noise

Effective Strategies for Standing out in Saturated Channels

In today's hyper-competitive world, every marketing channel feels like a crowded room with everyone shouting at once. Standing out isn't just about being seen—it's about making a meaningful impact that lingers in your audience's minds long after the initial interaction. The secret lies in blending creativity, strategy, and consistency to rise above the noise and connect with your audience on a deeper level. Here's how you can achieve that by diving into strategies that don't just attract attention but hold it.

1. Know Your Audience (Like, Really Know Them)

Understanding your audience is the cornerstone of effective marketing. Generic messaging gets lost in the shuffle, but when you take the time to understand your audience's needs, desires, and challenges, you can create campaigns that resonate deeply. This goes beyond basic demographics—it's about diving into psychographics, behaviors, and even quirks. The better you know your audience, the more effectively you can segment them into meaningful groups and tailor your messages to their unique preferences. Personalized campaigns make your audience feel seen and understood, which naturally draws them in and sets you apart from competitors.

2. Tell a Story They Can't Ignore

Storytelling isn't just a buzzword—it's a powerful way to engage your audience emotionally. Stories create context, meaning, and relatability, making your brand more than just a business; they make it human. A strong story is memorable because it taps into emotions like joy, aspiration, or even nostalgia. Think about your brand's journey, its mission, or the impact it has had on people's lives. Craft narratives that put your customer at the heart of the story and show how your brand plays a meaningful role in their journey. A compelling story isn't just heard—it's felt and shared.

3. Be Bold and Unforgettable

Blending in is a surefire way to get lost in the crowd. To stand out, you need to take calculated risks in how you present your brand. Boldness can come from using eye-catching visuals, an unconventional tone of voice, or surprising your audience with unexpected campaigns. Boldness grabs attention, but the key is to ensure that it aligns with your brand's identity and doesn't feel forced. Being bold is about pushing boundaries in a way that feels authentic, making your brand memorable for all the right reasons.

4. Go Where Your Competitors Aren't

Saturation in popular channels can make it hard for your message to cut through the clutter. Instead of competing in the same crowded spaces, explore underutilized platforms or channels. Look for opportunities in niche markets, alternative media, or emerging technologies that allow you to connect with your audience without the noise of heavy competition. Being an early adopter or exploring unconventional spaces can give your brand the visibility it needs to stand apart.

5. Focus on Value, Not Volume

The number of ads you put out isn't what makes your brand stand out—it's the value those ads provide. Instead of overwhelming your audience with constant noise, focus on creating high-quality content that informs, entertains, or solves a problem.

When you provide real value, your audience will naturally gravitate toward your brand. Value-driven marketing builds trust, establishes authority, and leaves a lasting impression that outshines flashy but hollow campaigns.

6. Leverage the Power of Communities

Communities are where authentic engagement happens. By being an active participant in spaces your audience cares about, you can build genuine connections that go beyond traditional marketing. Communities allow your brand to become part of the conversation, showing your audience that you're invested in what they value. Whether you're creating your own community or joining an existing one, these spaces foster loyalty and make your brand a trusted voice in the dialogue.

7. Be Consistent Across Channels

Consistency builds recognition, trust, and credibility. When your brand's voice, visuals, and messaging are cohesive across all platforms, it reinforces your identity in your audience's mind. Inconsistent branding, on the other hand, can confuse or alienate your audience. Your brand should feel familiar no matter where or how people interact with it. From social media posts to email campaigns and in-store experiences, ensure every touchpoint aligns with your overarching identity.

8. Leverage Real-Time Marketing

Staying timely and relevant is one of the most effective ways to cut through the noise. Real-time marketing allows you to engage with your audience during cultural moments, trending topics, or major events. However, this strategy requires agility and authenticity. Real-time campaigns should feel organic and align with your brand's personality, ensuring they don't come across as opportunistic or forced. When executed well, real-time marketing makes your brand feel alive and engaged with the world.

9. Invest in Emotional Connections

Emotions are the glue that holds your audience's attention and keeps them coming back. By tapping into universal feelings like happiness, inspiration, or even vulnerability, your campaigns can create deeper bonds with your audience. Emotional connections go beyond product features—they show your audience that your brand understands and cares about their needs, aspirations, and values. This emotional resonance makes your brand unforgettable and fosters loyalty over time.

10. Measure and Adapt

The marketing landscape changes constantly, and the strategies that work today might not work tomorrow. To stay ahead, you need to measure the performance of your campaigns and adapt based on what you learn. Analytics tools can provide insights into what's resonating with your audience and where you're falling short. By constantly iterating and refining your approach, you ensure your marketing stays effective and relevant, allowing your brand to continually stand out.

Standing out in saturated channels isn't about shouting louder—it's about creating a meaningful, authentic connection with your audience. By understanding their needs, telling compelling stories, embracing boldness, and delivering value, you can rise above the noise and make your brand unforgettable. Combine this with consistency, emotional resonance, and a willingness to adapt, and you have a recipe for cutting through the chaos and capturing your audience's attention in ways that truly matter.

Influencer Marketing and Unconventional Campaigns

The Power of Influencer Marketing

Influencers are the storytellers of the digital age. They have built loyal followings by sharing relatable content, authentic experiences, and a touch of their unique personality. When brands collaborate with influencers, they tap into these trusted voices to deliver messages that feel organic rather than forced.

The magic of influencer marketing lies in its ability to bridge the gap between brands and their audience. Unlike traditional ads, influencer campaigns feel personal—like a friend recommending a product they genuinely love. This authenticity builds trust and makes the audience more likely to engage with the brand.

To make influencer marketing work, brands must choose partners wisely. It's not about who has the most followers; it's about who aligns with your brand's values, tone, and audience. Micro-influencers, for instance, often have smaller but highly engaged communities, making their recommendations even more impactful. Whether it's a beauty guru reviewing skincare or a fitness enthusiast showcasing activewear, the key is authenticity—both in the influencer's voice and the brand's messaging.

Unconventional Campaigns: Thinking Outside the Box

Unconventional campaigns are all about breaking rules and surprising audiences. They challenge norms, take creative risks, and make people stop and pay attention. These campaigns don't just advertise—they entertain, inspire, or provoke thought, making them inherently shareable and memorable.

Unconventional campaigns often work because they catch people off guard. Whether it's a flash mob in a shopping mall or a billboard that changes with the weather, these unexpected elements create buzz and excitement. The surprise factor draws people in, encouraging them to share the experience with their friends and on social media.

Giving your audience a chance to participate in your campaign can create deeper connections. From gamified apps to pop-up installations, interactive campaigns let people engage with your brand in a tangible way. These experiences turn your audience into active participants, making your campaign not just seen but felt.

The most unconventional campaigns often tap into emotions—whether it's humor, nostalgia, or empathy. Emotional resonance makes campaigns memorable and fosters a stronger bond with the audience. When people feel something, they're more likely to share it and remember your brand.

Combining Influencer Marketing with Unconventional Campaigns

The real magic happens when influencer marketing and unconventional campaigns join forces. By involving influencers in bold, unexpected campaigns, you amplify their reach and authenticity. Influencers bring their loyal followers to the table, while the unconventional nature of the campaign ensures it grabs attention.

For instance, a brand launching a new product could create an immersive experience—a treasure hunt, a themed event, or a viral challenge—and involve influencers to lead the charge. The influencers' followers are naturally drawn into the campaign, creating organic buzz that spreads far beyond the original audience.

Influencer marketing and unconventional campaigns are powerful tools for cutting through the noise and making your brand stand out. They rely on authenticity, creativity, and emotional engagement to capture attention and foster connections. By embracing these strategies and executing them thoughtfully, your brand can not only rise above the chaos but also leave a lasting impression on your audience. So, think big, take risks, and let your creativity shine—it's time to make your mark!

The Psychology and Science of Branding

CHAPTER SIXTEEN

The Neuroscience of Branding

Understanding How Consumers Process and Remember Brands

Branding isn't just about creating logos or catchy slogans—it's about embedding your brand into the minds of consumers in a way that sticks. To achieve this, it's essential to understand the neuroscience behind how consumers process and remember brands. The human brain is wired to make quick decisions, often based on emotions and past experiences, and your brand has just a few seconds to make an impression. So, how do you ensure your brand not only gets noticed but also becomes unforgettable?

How the Brain Processes Brands?

The brain is a pattern-seeking machine, constantly processing visual, auditory, and emotional cues to make sense of the world. When consumers encounter a brand, their brains are working overtime, processing everything from colors and fonts to tone of voice and messaging. This sensory input gets categorized into existing mental frameworks—or "schemas"—that help the brain decide whether to engage with or ignore the brand.

For example, a fast-food brand might evoke memories of quick meals and childhood treats, while a luxury brand might trigger associations with exclusivity and elegance. The key is to create branding elements that align with the emotional response you want to evoke. The more consistent and clear these cues are, the easier it is for the brain to recognize and remember your brand.

The Role of Emotion in Branding

Emotion is the secret of memorable brands. Neuroscience reveals that emotional experiences activate the brain's limbic system, which plays a crucial role in memory formation. In simpler terms, people remember how you make them feel.

When a brand triggers joy, nostalgia, excitement, or even empathy, it creates a powerful emotional imprint. Think about the warm, fuzzy feeling associated with holiday ads or the adrenaline rush tied to sports brand campaigns. These emotions are stored alongside the brand, making it more likely to be recalled later.

Brands that consistently evoke positive emotions create loyalty that goes beyond rational decision-making. This is why emotional storytelling, whether through advertising, social media, or customer experiences, is so effective.

How Consumers Remember Brands?

1. Repetition and Familiarity

Repetition strengthens neural connections, making it easier for consumers to recognize and recall your brand. This is why consistency across all touchpoints—logos, taglines, colors, and messaging—is crucial. The more familiar your brand feels, the more likely it is to be remembered.

2. Distinctiveness

The brain is drawn to novelty and things that stand out. A unique logo, bold design, or unconventional approach can break through the mental clutter and grab attention. However, the challenge is to balance uniqueness with familiarity to ensure your brand is memorable for the right reasons.

3. Association

The brain uses associations to connect new information with existing memories. Strong branding leverages this by linking your brand to relatable ideas, emotions, or experiences. For instance, a health-conscious brand might associate itself with vitality and energy, creating a mental shortcut for consumers to remember it.

4. Simplicity

The brain loves simplicity. Overcomplicated designs, messaging, or visuals can overwhelm consumers and make your brand harder to remember. Clear, concise branding elements are easier for the brain to process and recall.

The Power of Visual and Sensory Branding

Visual cues, like colors, shapes, and typography, play a huge role in how brands are processed and remembered. The brain processes images faster than text, which is why logos, packaging, and visual content are so impactful.

For example, colors evoke specific emotions—red can signal passion or urgency, while blue conveys trust and calm. Similarly, fonts can communicate personality: playful, formal, bold, or approachable. By carefully choosing your visual elements, you can influence how consumers perceive your brand.

But branding isn't limited to visuals. Sensory elements like sound, texture, and even scent can create deeper connections. The jingle of a brand, the texture of its packaging, or the scent of its stores can all trigger powerful memories. The more senses your brand engages, the more memorable it becomes.

Building Brand Loyalty Through Neuroscience

Neuroscience also sheds light on how to foster loyalty. Repeated positive experiences with a brand activate the brain's reward system, releasing dopamine—a feel-good neurotransmitter. Over time, this creates a habit loop: consumers associate your brand with positive feelings and keep coming back for more.

Loyalty is also reinforced by trust. When a brand consistently delivers on its promises, the brain categorizes it as reliable, making it a go-to choice. Transparency, quality, and exceptional customer experiences all play a role in building this trust.

Practical Tips for Leveraging Neuroscience in Branding

- **Be Consistent**

- **Evoke Emotion**
- **Engage the Senses**
- **Simplify**
- **Tell a Story**

The neuroscience of branding reveals that consumers don't just see or hear your brand—they experience it. By understanding how the brain processes and remembers brands, you can create an identity that resonates emotionally, engages the senses, and stays top of mind. Whether it's through consistent visuals, emotional storytelling, or memorable sensory experiences, the key is to create a brand that feels impossible to forget. So, tap into the power of the brain, and watch as your brand becomes an unforgettable part of your customers' lives.

Leveraging Cognitive Psychology for Better Positioning

Branding is basically a game of mind tricks—the good kind, of course. It's about understanding how people's brains tick, so you can cozy up in their mental real estate and never leave. To start, first impressions are everything. The brain makes snap judgments faster than you can say "tagline," so your logo, colors, and tone need to scream, "Hey, I'm worth your attention!" Simplicity wins here—if people have to squint to understand your message, you've already lost. The brain loves things that are easy to process, and this is where cognitive fluency shines. Clear, consistent branding feels like comfort food to the mind—it's instantly recognizable and oh-so-inviting.

Then there's emotion, the secret sauce of memory. Neuroscience tells us that people might forget your product's specs, but they'll never forget how you made them feel. Whether it's joy, nostalgia, or a warm fuzzy feeling, brands that tug at heartstrings stick around in those neural pathways. Add a killer story to the mix, and you've got a one-way ticket to long-term brand loyalty. But don't stop there! Use the halo effect—when you excel in one area (say, product quality), people naturally assume you're nailing everything else, too (like customer service). Hello, instant trust boost!

Speaking of trust, social proof is your golden ticket. Humans are wired to follow the herd, so showcasing glowing reviews, testimonials, or influencer shout-outs makes your brand the one they want to bet on. Pair this with repetition—because let's face it, the brain loves a good encore—and your brand becomes unforgettable. Just make sure your messaging doesn't feel like an overplayed song. Sprinkle in the scarcity principle ("only a few left!") for some urgency, but keep it real—nobody likes a brand that cries wolf.

Even pricing can play Jedi mind tricks. Anchor high prices first, and suddenly, your regular offerings seem like a steal. And when customers finally make a purchase, keep the love alive with post-buy affirmations like follow-ups or pro tips, soothing any cognitive dissonance and reinforcing that they made the right choice.

So, what's the key takeaway here? Brands that leverage cognitive psychology know how to whisper sweet nothings to the brain. They're simple, emotional, trustworthy, and unforgettable—like that catchy song you can't stop humming. Play it smart, and your brand won't just be noticed—it'll be loved, remembered, and obsessively chosen.

CHAPTER SEVENTEEN

THE POWER OF EMOTIONAL TRIGGERS

How Emotions Influence Purchasing Decisions

Most of us don't shop with our heads—we shop with our hearts. Sure, we tell ourselves we're being practical, but deep down, it's the thrill, nostalgia, or even a pinch of FOMO that makes us hit "Buy Now." This isn't just a theory; it's science! Our brains are wired to react emotionally before they even begin to process logic. That's why we don't just see products—we feel them. And brands that know how to pull those emotional strings? They're the ones that win us over, not just for a moment but often for a lifetime.

Take joy, for example—it's the MVP of emotional triggers. Think about how good it feels to open a beautifully wrapped package or see an ad that makes you laugh out loud. That burst of happiness sticks in your brain, creating a warm, fuzzy association with the brand. It's why ads with adorable puppies, hilarious jokes, or uplifting music work so well. They're not just selling products—they're selling smiles. And let's be honest, who doesn't want a little more joy in their life?

Now, let's talk about FOMO, the sneaky little devil of marketing. Nothing gets your adrenaline pumping like a "limited-time offer" or "only 2 left in stock!" It's not just urgency—it's the fear that if you don't act now, you'll miss out forever. Your brain can barely handle it. Suddenly, you're in a race against time (and other shoppers) to snag that deal. Even if you didn't need a new coffee maker five minutes ago, the thought of someone else getting the last one makes you whip out your credit card faster than you can say "express shipping."

And then there's nostalgia, the marketing equivalent of comfort food. Brands know that tugging at your heartstrings with a hint of the past is a surefire way to get you onboard. Retro packaging, throwback campaigns, and classic jingles don't just remind you of the good old days—they make you feel them. That's why reboots of old TV shows, vintage-inspired sneakers, or anything that screams "remember this?" are irresistible. Nostalgia turns shopping into a time machine, taking you back to simpler, happier moments, and that emotional connection makes your decision to buy feel personal.

But it's not all about happiness and nostalgia—trust and safety are emotional heavyweights too. In a world full of scams and shady deals, finding a brand you trust feels like a breath of fresh air. Whether it's a small business that's transparent about its practices or a big company that delivers on its promises, trust is what keeps customers coming back. It's why certifications, ethical sourcing, and honest customer service matter so much. When a brand feels reliable, it's like a friend you can always count on—and who doesn't want more friends like that?

Aspiration is another emotional powerhouse. It's that little voice in your head saying, "This could be you." Whether it's a sleek sports car, a designer handbag, or even a subscription to an online course, aspirational brands don't just sell products—they sell dreams. They give you a glimpse of your ideal self, whether it's cooler, smarter, or more accomplished. And let's be real, we all love to indulge in a bit of daydreaming, especially if it comes with a shiny new gadget or outfit.

Empathy and compassion also pack a punch in the emotional branding world. When a brand aligns itself with causes that matter—whether it's environmental sustainability, fighting hunger, or supporting marginalized communities—it creates a sense of purpose. Buying their product feels like doing your part to make the world a better place, and that emotional satisfaction is hard to resist. Suddenly, a reusable water bottle or a pair of shoes isn't just an item—it's a statement.

Now, let's get into how brands put all these emotions to work. It starts with creating memorable experiences. Whether it's a delightfully quirky ad campaign or a customer service interaction that leaves you smiling, these moments build a reservoir of positive feelings associated with the brand. It's why unboxing videos are such a phenomenon—brands that focus on the experience, from the packaging to the product itself, make you feel like you're unwrapping a gift, not just a purchase.

Storytelling takes it up another notch. People are hardwired to connect with stories, especially ones that feel authentic and relatable. A brand's story about overcoming obstacles, supporting a cause, or making a customer's life better doesn't just inform—it inspires. When you see yourself in a brand's story, it feels personal, and that emotional connection turns into loyalty.

Visual and sensory cues also do a lot of heavy lifting. Colors, sounds, and even textures can evoke strong emotional responses. Bright, warm colors like red and yellow spark excitement and energy, while cooler tones like blue and green create feelings of trust and calm. Pair that with a catchy jingle or a comforting scent, and you've got a sensory experience that sticks. These little details might seem small, but they're what make a brand memorable in the long run.

Personalization is another key player in emotional branding. When a brand remembers your preferences, sends you birthday discounts, or recommends something you didn't even know you wanted, it feels like they truly "get" you. That feeling of being seen and valued creates an emotional bond that goes beyond just liking a product—it makes you loyal to the brand itself.

But here's the thing—emotional triggers only work when they're authentic. Customers can smell manipulation a mile away, and overdoing it can make your brand come off as insincere. The trick is to align your emotional appeals with your brand's core values and mission. When emotions are used thoughtfully and genuinely, they're not just a way to sell—they're a way to connect.

So, the next time you're drawn to a brand or product without fully understanding why, remember: it's not just what they're selling—it's how they're making you feel. Whether it's joy, trust, nostalgia, or FOMO, emotions are the secret sauce that turns casual shoppers into loyal fans. Brands that master emotional triggers don't just thrive—they create lasting impressions that keep customers coming back, again and again. And honestly, who can say no to that?

Designing Brands That Evoke Lasting Feelings

Great brands don't just sell products; they make you feel something. Whether it's the comfort of a warm hug, the thrill of possibility, or the nostalgia of simpler times, emotional branding goes far beyond logos and taglines—it taps into the very heart of human experience. When you design a brand that evokes lasting feelings, you're not just building a business; you're crafting a relationship that sticks in the minds and hearts of your audience.

How to Design a Brand That Evokes Lasting Feelings?

1. Start with Your Core Values

A brand's emotional resonance begins with its values. What does your brand stand for? Is it about inspiring confidence, delivering joy, or fostering belonging? Your values should guide every aspect of your design—from your logo to your messaging. If your brand exudes authenticity and sticks to its values, customers will naturally feel connected to it.

2. Use Colors That Speak Volumes

Colors are emotional shortcuts. The right palette can evoke specific feelings instantly. Warm tones like red and orange create energy and passion, while cool tones like blue and green bring calmness and trust. The key is to choose colors that align with the emotions you want your brand to evoke. Think of your palette as the emotional backdrop of your brand—it sets the tone before you say a single word.

3. Craft a Logo That Resonates

Your logo is often the first interaction a customer has with your brand, so it needs to hit the right emotional notes. A minimalist logo might evoke sophistication, while a playful one feels approachable and fun. The shape of your logo matters too: rounded designs feel friendly and comforting, while angular shapes evoke strength and reliability.

4. Write Copy That Feels Like a Conversation

Words have power, and your brand's tone of voice should feel like a conversation with your audience. If your brand is playful, your copy should make people smile or laugh. If it's empathetic, your words should feel like a friend's advice on a tough day. The goal is to use language that creates an emotional connection, whether it's through humor, reassurance, or inspiration.

5. Tell Stories That Stick

Humans are wired to remember stories, not facts. Brands that weave compelling narratives create lasting emotional impressions. Share your journey, spotlight customer success stories, or highlight the real-world impact of your work. The more relatable and heartfelt your stories, the deeper the emotional connection they'll foster.

6. Create Sensory Experiences

Emotions are tied to the senses, so designing multisensory experiences can elevate your brand's emotional impact. A signature scent, a catchy jingle, or even a specific texture in your packaging can create associations that make your brand unforgettable. When customers experience your brand through multiple senses, it embeds deeper in their memory.

7. Be Consistent Across Touchpoints

Emotional resonance requires repetition and reinforcement. Your website, social media, packaging, and in-store experience should all evoke the same feelings. Consistency across touchpoints ensures that customers recognize and trust your brand, no matter where they encounter it.

Designing a brand that evokes lasting feelings is both an art and a science. By understanding the emotional triggers that resonate with your audience, you can create a brand that not only attracts attention but also builds loyalty. From thoughtful visuals and heartfelt stories to consistent touchpoints and sensory elements, every aspect of your brand should aim to make an emotional impact. After all, customers may forget what you said or sold—but they'll always remember how your brand made them feel.

CHAPTER EIGHTEEN

Cultural and Behavioral Insights

Aligning with Cultural Trends and Societal Shifts

Honestly—trends rule the world. Whether it's the latest TikTok dance craze or society's growing focus on sustainability, cultural trends and societal shifts shape how people think, act, and spend. Smart brands don't just follow these shifts; they align with them to stay relevant and resonate with their audience. It's not about being trendy for the sake of it—it's about genuinely reflecting the values and priorities of the time.

Take the rise of sustainability, for example. Consumers are increasingly choosing brands that prioritize eco-friendly practices, and aligning with this trend doesn't just win you points; it builds trust. But here's the catch: you can't fake it. Jumping on a trend without authenticity—like slapping a "green" label on a product without actual sustainability efforts—will backfire faster than you can say "greenwashing." Instead, make societal alignment part of your brand's DNA.

Then there's inclusivity, another cultural wave reshaping the branding world. Customers want to see themselves reflected in ads, products, and campaigns, and they're quick to call out brands that don't deliver. By celebrating diversity and showing real-world representation, brands can build deeper connections with broader audiences. It's not just a box to check—it's about genuinely understanding your audience's lived experiences and making them feel seen and valued.

Aligning with cultural trends also requires agility. Trends can change overnight, and societal conversations evolve quickly. Brands that keep their finger on the pulse—through social listening, market research, and cultural observation—can adapt their messaging and strategies to stay relevant. But remember, it's a fine balance. Being authentic and intentional is far more impactful than jumping on every viral moment.

Ultimately, aligning with cultural trends and societal shifts is about understanding your audience on a deeper level. It's about tapping into their values, addressing their concerns, and showing them that your brand isn't just selling products—it's part of the bigger conversation. When done right, it's not just marketing; it's a movement.

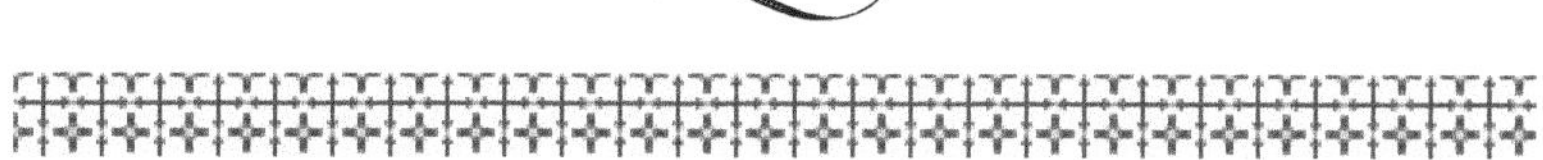

Localizing Your Brand for Global Markets

Ah, the beauty of globalization—it lets your brand reach new corners of the world, but here's the twist: what works in one market might flop spectacularly in another. That's where localization comes in. It's the art of tailoring your brand to fit the cultural, linguistic, and behavioral nuances of a specific market. Think of it like hosting a dinner party in a new country—you wouldn't serve the same dish everywhere, would you? You'd adapt to local tastes and traditions.

Localization isn't just about translating your tagline into a new language (though, please, get that right too). It's about capturing the essence of a culture and weaving it into your brand. This means understanding local customs, values, and humor. A joke that kills in New York might get blank stares in Tokyo, and a color scheme that feels festive in one culture might signal mourning in another. Paying attention to these subtleties ensures your brand feels thoughtful and relatable.

But it's not just about avoiding faux pas—it's about making people feel like your brand belongs. Using local idioms, featuring regional landmarks in your campaigns, or collaborating with homegrown influencers makes your brand feel like part of the community, not an outsider trying to fit in. It's like saying, "We see you, and we get you," and that connection is priceless.

Localization also extends to your product or service. What customers crave in one country might differ dramatically in another. For instance, offering spicy food options in markets that love heat or adjusting your clothing line for regional climates shows that you've done your homework. It's the little touches that show your brand cares about its audience's unique needs.

Of course, localization has its challenges. It requires research, investment, and sometimes, letting go of global consistency to embrace local uniqueness. But the payoff? A brand that doesn't just survive in new markets—it thrives. When customers see a brand making the effort to connect with their culture, they're more likely to embrace it as their own.

In the end, localization is about respect and understanding. It's about meeting your audience where they are—on their terms, in their language, and with their traditions in mind. So, go ahead: explore the world, but don't forget to pack a little cultural sensitivity.

Building a Legacy of Distinction

CHAPTER NINETEEN

The Beyond Vanilla Manifesto

In a world overflowing with options, mediocrity is your greatest enemy. Your brand isn't here to blend in; it's here to stand out, to be the choice that turns heads, sparks conversations, and leaves a mark. The Beyond Vanilla Manifesto is a call to action for brands ready to embrace their individuality and craft experiences that go beyond the ordinary. It's a set of principles to guide you as you step boldly into your unique identity and inspire others along the way.

Principles for Maintaining Exceptionalism

1. Authenticity First

Being exceptional starts with being real. Your brand's power lies in its story, values, and unique quirks—don't water them down to please the masses. Stay true to who you are, even when it feels risky. Authenticity resonates because it's rare, and rare things are unforgettable.

2. Obsess Over the Details

Exceptional brands know that greatness is in the details. From the texture of your packaging to the tone of your email greetings, every touchpoint should reflect the care and creativity you pour into your brand. The little things are what turn ordinary moments into extraordinary experiences.

3. Stay Curious, Stay Bold

Exceptionalism thrives on curiosity. Ask questions, challenge norms, and explore the "what ifs." Boldness doesn't mean being loud—it means daring to be different. Exceptional brands aren't afraid to experiment, fail, and try again.

4. Evolve, but Stay Grounded

The world moves fast, and so should your brand. But while trends change, your values are your anchor. Evolve thoughtfully, ensuring that every pivot or rebrand feels like a natural extension of your core identity, not a departure from it.

5. Delight and Surprise

Exceptional brands make people smile, gasp, or stop in their tracks. They deliver joy when it's least expected. Surprise your customers with thoughtful gestures, clever campaigns, or extra perks that make them feel valued.

6. Listen, Learn, and Adapt

Exceptionalism isn't a one-and-done deal—it's a constant journey. Listen to your customers, embrace feedback, and adapt to meet their needs. The best brands aren't static; they're dynamic, always improving and evolving.

7. Lead with Purpose

Exceptional brands don't just sell—they stand for something. Whether it's sustainability, inclusivity, or creativity, your purpose should be woven into everything you do. A strong sense of purpose inspires loyalty and sets your brand apart from the pack.

Inspiring Words for Brands on Their Journey to Uniqueness

Dear brand,

You weren't made to be forgettable. The world doesn't need another "good enough" option or a copycat of what's already out there. It needs you—bold, unapologetic, and uniquely yourself.

Your journey to exceptionalism won't always be easy. There will be moments when playing it safe feels tempting, when the pressure to conform whispers in your ear. Resist it. Greatness lies in your willingness to take risks, to celebrate your individuality, and to show up with unwavering confidence in what makes you different.

Remember, exceptionalism isn't about perfection—it's about passion. It's about the energy you bring, the story you tell, and the connections you build. It's about surprising people, delighting them, and reminding them why your brand is unlike any other.

So, embrace your quirks, own your story, and step boldly into your uniqueness. The world is watching, waiting to see what only you can bring to the table.

This is your manifesto. This is your moment. Go beyond vanilla—and never look back.

With courage and creativity,
The Beyond Vanilla Manifesto

CHAPTER TWENTY

FUTURE-PROOFING YOUR BRAND

Adapting to New Technologies and Market Dynamics

The rise of new technologies has completely transformed how businesses connect with their audiences. From artificial intelligence to augmented reality, the tools at our disposal feel like they've jumped straight out of a sci-fi movie. But here's the kicker—they're not futuristic dreams; they're here, now, and constantly evolving. To future-proof your brand, you've got to embrace a mindset of curiosity, learning, and adaptability. Think of it like riding a rollercoaster—scary at times, but oh-so exhilarating if you lean into the twists and turns.

First, let's talk about embracing emerging technologies. AI, blockchain, AR/VR—they're not just buzzwords; they're game-changers. AI can tailor recommendations that feel like your brand is reading customers' minds (in a good way, of course). Chatbots? They've gone from clunky robots to smooth conversationalists that make customer service available 24/7. And AR? It's making shopping an experience—customers can now "try on" sunglasses or see how a couch looks in their living room without leaving their homes. The trick isn't to use every shiny new tool—it's to pick the ones that elevate what makes your brand special.

But technology is only half the story—staying agile is where the magic happens. Market trends can change faster than a viral TikTok challenge, and brands that cling too tightly to "the way we've always done it" risk being left behind. Being agile means being ready to pivot, whether it's adjusting your product lineup, tweaking your marketing message, or suddenly finding a new distribution channel because that's where your audience is hanging out. Flexibility isn't just a nice-to-have; it's your survival strategy in a world where change is the only constant.

Never underestimate the power of keeping an eye on the competition. Watching what others are doing isn't about copying—it's about learning. What tech are they experimenting with? What strategies are taking off in your industry? And, let's be honest, what missteps can you avoid thanks to their bold (but failed) experiments? Staying clued in helps you spot opportunities to innovate and keeps your brand sharp, relevant, and one step ahead.

In this fast-paced world, the brands that thrive aren't the ones that wait for the future to arrive—they're the ones already building it. So grab the tech reins, stay nimble, and keep your eyes peeled for what's next. The future doesn't wait, but with the right mindset, your brand will be ready for anything.

Anticipating Consumer Needs in a Fast-Changing World

The brands that thrive are the ones that anticipate what customers want before they know they want it. This requires a deep understanding of human behavior, cultural trends, and emerging societal shifts.

1. Listen Actively

Your customers are constantly telling you what they need—through reviews, social media, and purchase behavior. Use these insights to stay ahead of the curve. Tools like social listening and sentiment analysis can help you identify patterns and trends in real-time, giving you a window into what's next.

2. Think Long-Term

Short-term wins are great, but future-proofing requires a long-term perspective. Anticipate how changes in technology, the economy, and culture might impact your industry in five, ten, or even twenty years. For example, sustainability is no longer just a trend—it's a long-term expectation. Brands that prioritize eco-friendly practices today are setting themselves up for success in a more environmentally conscious future.

3. Innovate With Purpose

Innovation for the sake of it can dilute your brand and confuse your audience. Instead, focus on innovations that solve real problems or improve the customer experience. Ask yourself: How does this new product, service, or feature make life better for my customers? The more aligned your innovation is with customer needs, the more likely it is to succeed.

4. Build Flexibility Into Your Operations

A fast-changing world demands flexible systems. From supply chain management to digital platforms, ensure your infrastructure can scale, pivot, and adapt as needed. Flexibility isn't just about surviving disruption—it's about leveraging it to your advantage.

> "*Future-Proofing in Action*
>
> *Future-proofing isn't just about big moves—it's also about the small, consistent actions that keep your brand resilient. Staying curious, embracing experimentation, and fostering a culture of innovation within your organization are all part of the process. By anticipating shifts in technology and consumer behavior, you position your brand as a leader, not a follower.*"

Future-proofing your brand isn't about predicting the future—it's about preparing for it. By staying adaptable, leveraging technology, and keeping a keen eye on consumer needs, you ensure your brand remains relevant and competitive, no matter how the world evolves. It's not just about surviving the next wave of change—it's about riding it with confidence and purpose. So, gear up, stay agile, and embrace the opportunities that lie ahead—because the future waits for no one.

CHAPTER TWENTY-ONE

Crafting Your Brand's Legacy

How to Stay Relevant and Admired for Generations

Building a brand legacy is like planting a tree: it takes time, care, and a whole lot of vision, but when done right, it becomes something majestic that people admire for years to come. Legacy isn't just about being remembered—it's about being remembered for the right reasons. It's about creating a brand that's not only relevant today but evolves gracefully with the times, staying true to its roots while branching out to meet new needs. Think of it as the ultimate balancing act: tradition meets innovation, and nostalgia meets forward-thinking.

First, let's talk roots. Your legacy starts with your core values—the "why" behind your brand. These are your non-negotiables, the things that define you no matter what changes. Maybe it's your commitment to quality, your dedication to sustainability, or your ability to make people laugh when they least expect it. Whatever it is, this is your foundation. Build it strong, and your brand will withstand storms of market trends, economic shifts, and generational changes.

But roots alone won't do. To stay relevant, you've got to **adapt**. Generations evolve, technologies change, and yesterday's "cool" can quickly become today's "cringe" if you're not paying attention. The brands that leave a legacy are the ones that keep listening and learning. They reinvent themselves without losing their essence, like that timeless friend who somehow makes every trend look effortless. Whether it's adopting new tech, speaking to fresh social movements, or tweaking your tone to match the times, flexibility is key to staying admired.

And don't forget to **inspire**. Legacy brands are more than businesses—they're movements. They create stories that people want to tell and memories they want to share. Think about the emotional impact your brand has—how does it make people feel? What kind of impact does it leave behind? Brands that inspire loyalty, joy, or even a sense of purpose don't just build customers; they build communities.

Finally, don't shy away from bold decisions. Legacy doesn't come from playing it safe—it comes from making waves. Stand for something meaningful, take risks when it counts, and never stop challenging the status quo. A legacy is about more than being remembered—it's about being unforgettable. So, plant those roots, reach for the sky, and craft a brand that people will admire for generations to come.

Brand Story: MyFroyoland

Premium Frozen Yogurt

The Birth of MyFroyoland

In the world of desserts, innovation is the key to staying ahead. MyFroyoland, a beloved brand that has become synonymous with frozen yogurt, is the perfect example of how an idea, rooted in simplicity, can evolve into a nationwide sensation. But how did this sweet success story begin?

The Inspiration behind MyFroyoland

It all started with a single, brilliant concept: frozen yogurt. While ice cream has long dominated the dessert market, frozen yogurt presented a healthier alternative that appealed to the growing health-conscious consumer. The founders of MyFroyoland recognized this gap in the market and saw an opportunity to create something that could satisfy both the sweet tooth and the need for better-for-you dessert options.

The idea wasn't just about frozen yogurt; it was about an **experience**. MyFroyoland wanted to offer something more than just a product—it wanted to give customers the ability to **personalize** their treat. The self-serve model allowed customers to express their creativity and create their own combinations, making each visit unique. This hands-on approach created a sense of connection with the product, and more importantly, a sense of ownership over their dessert.

The Vision and Mission of the Brand

At its core, MyFroyoland was built on the idea of **freedom of choice** and **joyful experience**. The founders set out with a clear vision: to offer a high-quality frozen yogurt experience that was fun, customizable, and accessible to everyone. This meant offering a wide variety of flavours, from rich chocolate hazelnut to refreshing fruit sorbets, and giving customers the ability to choose their own toppings, allowing for endless combinations.

But there was more to it. MyFroyoland's mission was not just to be a place where people could treat themselves, but to also contribute to the health-conscious movement by offering options like **sugar-free**, **dairy-free**, and gut-friendly frozen yogurt. This focus on **quality** and **health** has been key in building the brand's loyal customer base.

Quality at the Core – Sourcing the Finest Ingredients

At MyFroyoland, quality is our top priority. To make sure every cup of frozen yogurt is as delicious as it is healthy, we only use the best ingredients, many of which come from **Australia**.

Premium Ingredients

Our yogurt starts with high-quality **milk** and **yogurt cultures** for the perfect creaminess and flavour. We also carefully select **fruits**, **nuts**, and **toppings** from trusted suppliers to ensure you're getting the best with every swirl. Whether you choose a classic flavour or try something new, you can trust that it's of the highest quality.

How It Differentiates Itself

What sets MyFroyoland apart from the competition is its commitment to **customization**. Many dessert brands offer pre-made options, but MyFroyoland gives the power to the customer. With a simple self-serve station, customers can load their yogurt with an array of toppings—from fresh fruit to chocolate sprinkles—and enjoy without the guilt.

The Journey from Inception to Expansion

From a small outlet to becoming a recognized brand across the world, MyFroyoland's journey has been one of innovation, resilience, and passion. As the company grew, so did its presence on social media, helping it connect with younger, tech-savvy customers who value personalization and convenience.

The brand's **consistent marketing efforts**—from Regional marketing, customer-centric campaigns, and brand collaborations —have helped it stay top-of-mind among customers, while its **Promotional Campaigns** keep people coming back for more.

MyFroyoland's ability to adapt to changing tastes and preferences while staying true to its roots of offering high-quality, customizable frozen yogurt has enabled it to stand out in an crowded market.

Crafting the MyFroyoland Experience

MyFroyoland isn't just about frozen yogurt – it's an experience. It's about discovering new flavours, customizing your treat, and enjoying it in a lively atmosphere.

Frozen Yogurt Bar

What makes MyFroyoland unique is our **self-serve concept**. You are the artist here! With many yogurt bases and a wide variety of toppings to choose from, every visit is an opportunity to create your perfect dessert. Whether you like something fruity and light or something richer, it's all up to you.

Store Ambience

When you walk into a MyFroyoland store, you'll feel immediately welcomed by a bright, friendly space designed to help you relax and enjoy your yogurt. From the modern design to the lively atmosphere, every detail is made with one goal: to offer the perfect place to enjoy your **premium frozen yogurt**.

Branding MyFroyoland – Making a Memorable Impact

A great brand connects with its customers, and MyFroyoland works hard to create a memorable experience that reflects our values of quality, fun, and personalization.

The Power of Colors and Logo

Our logo uses a **vibrant pink** to represent fun and energy, while the **blue** adds a sense of freshness and calm. This colorful design ensures that MyFroyoland stands out, whether you're just passing by or browsing online.

Tagline and Messaging

Our tagline, "**Premium Frozen Yogurt**", perfectly reflects our commitment to providing high-quality frozen yogurt that tastes amazing and meets health-conscious needs. Our messaging focuses on making every yogurt experience special – not just a treat, but a premium experience.

Innovation and Adaptability – Evolving with Trends

The world of food trends moves quickly, and MyFroyoland stays ahead by always innovating. We adapt our menu to meet the changing tastes and preferences of our customers.

Seasonal flavours and Limited Editions

To keep things exciting, we offer new **seasonal** and **limited-edition** flavours of yogurt options throughout the year. Whether it's a refreshing summer flavour or a cozy winter special, we always have something fresh and exciting to try.

Customer-Centric Approach – Building Long-Lasting Relationships

At MyFroyoland, we don't just serve frozen yogurt – we build relationships. We want every customer to feel like part of the MyFroyoland family.

Loyalty Programs

Our loyalty app is now available, rewarding our regular customers with points on every purchase, special discounts, and birthday rewards. We launched it on February 6th, the same day as International Frozen Yogurt Day!

Personalized Service

At MyFroyoland, we believe in giving you the freedom to create your perfect treat. While you're in control of choosing your favorite flavours and toppings, our staff is always there to guide and assist, ensuring your experience is smooth and enjoyable. We want every visit to feel special, and our goal is to make you feel like you're a valued member of the MyFroyoland community.

Building Strong Community Ties – MyFroyoland's Commitment to Regional Engagement

We believe in giving back to the communities we serve. At MyFroyoland, we're committed to building strong relationships with regional customers and causes.

Corporate Social Responsibility

We regularly participate in charity events, donating part of our profits to local causes. Whether it's supporting the environment or local schools, MyFroyoland is dedicated to making a positive impact in the community.

Hosting Events and Collaborations

We love bringing people together. Whether it's a **flavour launch party**, a **wellness workshop**, or a **customer appreciation day**, we host events to celebrate and engage with our customers. We also work with local businesses to showcase talent and build stronger community connections.

Eco-Friendly Initiatives

Sustainability is important to us. MyFroyoland uses **eco-friendly packaging**, minimizes waste, and partners with environmental groups to reduce our carbon footprint. Our goal is to offer a delicious treat while being mindful of the planet.

Conclusion: A Brand Built on Quality, Innovation, and Community

MyFroyoland isn't just a frozen yogurt store – it's a brand that stands for **premium frozen yogurt**, **customization**, and **community**. Every cup of yogurt we serve brings our values to life, creating an experience our customers love. As we continue to grow, we remain committed to offering the best: the finest ingredients, innovative flavours, and customer-focused service.

Worksheets And Exercises For Immediate Action

Worksheets

Worksheet 1: The Brand Identity Map

This exercise is all about figuring out who you are. Grab a piece of paper or open a document and jot down the following:

Core Values: What does your brand stand for? Is it innovation, sustainability, humor, trust? List at least three.

Mission: What's your "why"? Why do you exist, and what change do you want to make in the world?

Audience: Who are you serving? Write down your ideal customer's demographics, interests, and pain points.

Voice: How do you want to sound? Friendly? Professional? Bold? Define your tone in three words.

Differentiator: What sets you apart? Is it your product, service, customer experience, or all three?

By the end, you'll have a clear snapshot of your brand's identity—your north star for all things unique.

Worksheet 2: The Competitor Spotlight

To stand out, you need to know what you're standing out from. This exercise helps you identify gaps in the market.

List Your Competitors: Write down the top 3-5 brands in your industry.

Study Their Strengths: What are they doing well? Note their standout features, customer reviews, and campaigns.

Spot Their Weaknesses: Where are they falling short? Look for gaps in their offerings, service, or messaging.

Find the Opportunity: Based on what you've uncovered, brainstorm ways your brand can fill the gap or do things differently.

Now, you're not just competing—you're outsmarting.

Worksheet 3: Action Planning Grid

Uniqueness isn't just about ideas—it's about execution. Use this grid to turn your insights into action:

TASK	OWNER	DEAD LINE	NEXT STEP
Define brand values	(Your Name)	(Date)	Finalise top 3-5 values
Create USP	(Your Name)	(Date)	Test pitches with team/audience
Launch new campaign	(Your Name)	(Date)	Draft concepts and visuals

Use this Grid as a Sample

Breaking it down ensures you stay on track and actually do the work to build your unique brand.

Exercises

Exercise 1: The Elevator Pitch Test

Can you describe your brand's uniqueness in 30 seconds? If not, it's time to refine your message. Practice answering these questions:

Who are you?

What do you do?

Why should people care?

Pro tip: Record yourself delivering your pitch and listen back. Does it sound exciting, clear, and memorable? If not, tweak until it does.

Exercise 2: The Customer Persona Builder

Understanding your audience is key to uniqueness. Create a detailed persona for your ideal customer:

Name and Background: Give them a name, age, and backstory.

Goals: What do they want to achieve?

Challenges: What's holding them back?

How You Help: How does your brand solve their problem or make their life better?

By visualizing your ideal customer, you can tailor your brand to meet their needs perfectly.

Exercise 3: Mood Board Magic

Visualizing your brand's vibe can spark fresh ideas. Gather images, colors, fonts, and textures that represent your brand. Use tools like Pinterest or Canva, or go old-school with a physical board. This exercise not only helps you see your brand's personality come to life but also ensures consistency in your design and messaging.

Other Books By The Author

Guide for investors seeking balance, growth & security

history and the way forward

SHAGUN JAIN

www.ingramcontent.com/pod-product-compliance
Lightning Source LLC
LaVergne TN
LVHW021153160826
845679LV00024B/2112

* 9 7 9 8 8 9 6 9 9 5 7 4 6 *